Lowry's Boats of Penzance

Painting of Traditional Vessels Associated with Mounts Bay, Cornwall

Roger Lowry

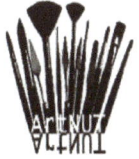

Roger Lowry

Copyright © Roger Lowry 2024

The right of Roger Lowry to be identified as the author of this work has been asserted in accordance with sections 77 and 78 of the Copyright Design and Patent Act 1988.

Published by ArtNut imprint of MA Publisher (Penzance)
Email: mapublisher@yahoo.com
Website: www.mapublisher.org.uk
Released on August 2024

Printed in the region the books have been published: Australia | Canada | Europe | UK | USA

ISBN-13: 978-1-915958105

All rights reserved. No part of this publication may be reproduced, stored in a retrieval system, or transmitted, in any form or by any means, electronic, mechanical, photocopying, recording, public performances or otherwise, without prior written permission of the copyright holder, except for brief quotations embodied in critical articles or reviews.

Disclaimer:
All expressions and opinions of the work belong to the artists and PA does not share or endorse any other than to provide the open platform to publish their work. For further information on PA policies please email: pennyauthors@yahoo.co.uk for furthor information and submission guidelines.

Cover designed by Mayar Akash
Cover image: by Roger Lowry (Penzance, Cornwall)
Typeset in Arial

Paper printed on is FSC Certified, lead free, acid free, buffered paper made from wood-based pulp. Our paper meets the ISO 9706 standard for permanent paper. As such, paper will last several hundred years when stored.

Dedication

She was gone already.

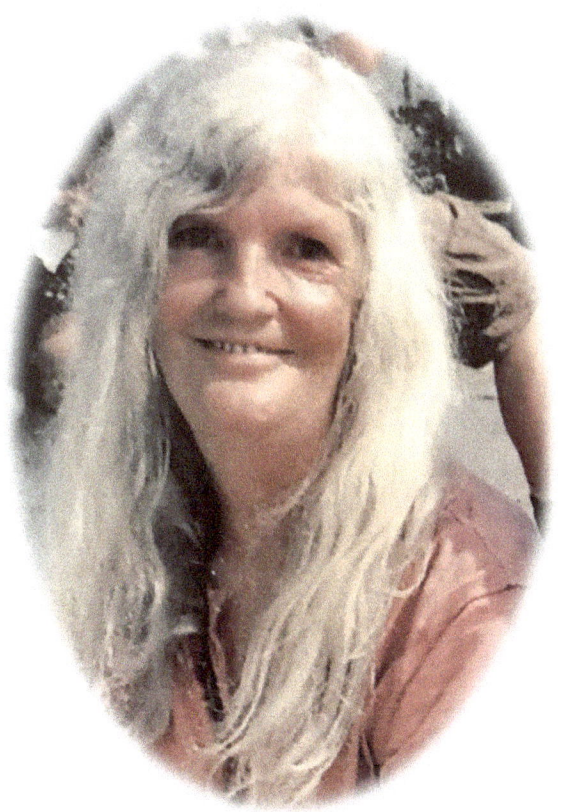

I painted the following image as a memorial.

It is titled "Out of This World", from a song by Tony Bennett in 1964.

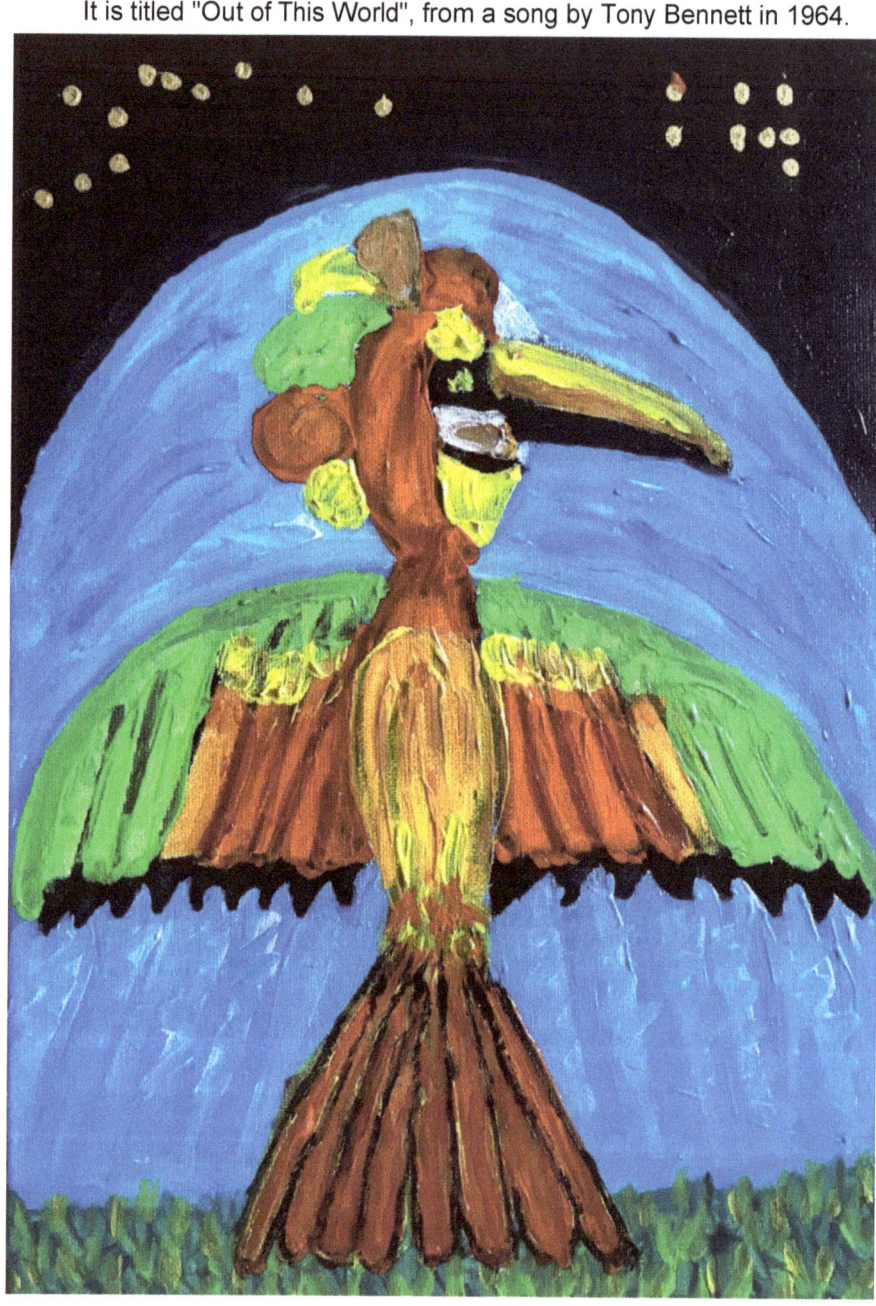

Acknowledgements

I would also like to thank the missus, Anne, for putting up with me while we went through this process.

I would like to thank Minnie for all her help.

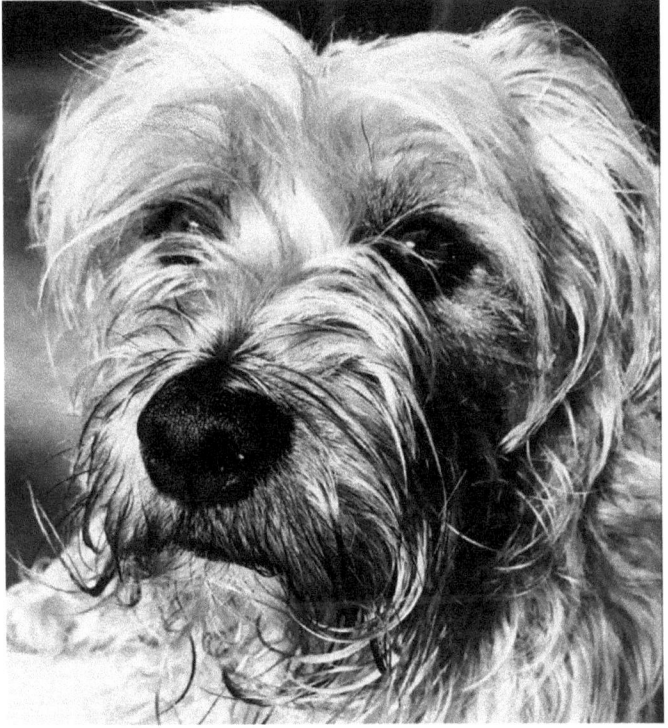

"Come on, get off that machine, I want to go walking!!"

Content

Dedication	3
Acknowledgements	5
Introduction	8
Abbey Basin	11
Asgaard 11	12
Astrid	13
Barnabas	14
Bessie Ellen & Pellew	15
Bessie Ellen	16
Blue Clipper	17
Breton Crabber	18
Captain Ahab	19
Carlos De Amesquita	20
Corydalis	21
Courier	22
Crazy Diamond	23
De Gallant	24
Dragon Fly	25
Dream Boat	26
Earl Of Pembroke	27
Elizabeth And Blanche	28
Ellian	29
Evening View	30
Excelsior	31
Eye Of The Wind	32
Feasible	33
Ghost Ship	34
Gleaner	35
Golden Hind	36
Grace	37
Grayhound	38
Grossheimherzogin Elisa	39
Gry Maritha	40
Guide Me	41
Gulliver	42
Happy Return	43
Happy Return	44
Hear The Sea	45
Herring Gull Story	46
Irene	47

Johanna Lucretia	48
John's Boys	49
Juno	50
Kara Mor And Karina Olsen	51
Kinsmen Of The Wind	52
Klevia	53
Lady Of Avenel	54
Le Belem	55
Little Gem And Minerva	56
Longship	57
Luggers Racing Off The Prom	58
Luke's Minnie	59
Mali Rose	60
Maria Assumpta	61
Matthew	62
Maybe 2021	63
Mayflower	64
Mez Creiz	65
Michael And Mary	66
Morning Light	67
Nordlys	68
Ocean Pride	69
Old Man Of The Sea	70
Orion	71
Pet	72
Penzance Harbour	73
Phoenix	74
Queen Of The Bay	75
Sv Nicolai	76
Thalassa	77
The Bag O' Rags	78
The Black Pig	79
Veryan In The Wet Dock	80
White Boat	81
Information Table	82
The Author	84
Book Review	85

Introduction

I was born in 1945, after the war in Europe ended and before the surrender of Japan, one of the last generation of a non-nuclear planet.

I left school in 1961 to work in the City of London at the office of the world's largest marine insurance broker. Unknown to me the school had entered one of my paintings, Bikers at the Ace Cafe, in a national competition run by one of the nation's newspapers. The painting was exhibited in the Royal Academy and I won a major prize. A camera for me and hundreds of pounds worth of art equipment and a framed print, Escaping Lines, by Paul Klee that hung on the wall outside the Headmasters office.

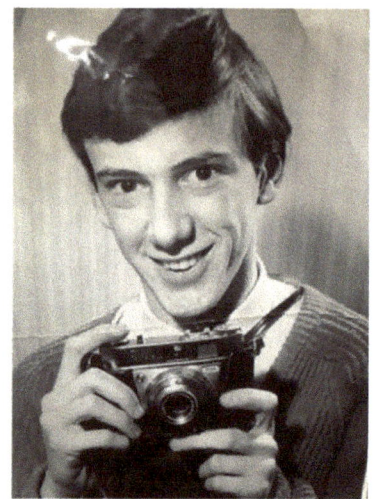

The official portrait for the prize giving

I took an interest in photography and built my own development room and didn't paint again for many years.

The city job ended when the management got miffed about me having time off to go to court after being arrested on CND demonstrations. I walked out into another job in the first credit company. It was owned and run by well off, well connected people with interesting lives. The manager was second lead violinist in the Royal Philharmonic Orchestra and also managed a leading opera singer.
The job made me rethink my life and I went on to work for a local authority parks department on trees and as a park keeper.

Holidays in Cornwall, and a little Celtic blood, caused me to move to a landscape where I felt I belonged. I did a bit of this and that to keep things together and met the missus in 1974. We moved in together in 1975. One of the bits was doing a four acre garden for the well connected, and that led me to Cornwall College doing horticulture. We were living in a barn in Sancreed at the time and had an allotment in Gulval growing our own and milking the landlady's goats to make cheese.

I passed the exams with flying colours and took a job managing a twelve acre garden with accommodation thrown in. That lasted a couple of years then I went self-employed landscaping etc. all over West Penwith.

We managed to buy a house in 1983 that we did up over winter. I did a bit of painting, The Divorce Party and one of us house sitting at Rinsey, but work was taking up to much time.

I was invited to become part of a co-operative that ran a nationally acclaimed alternative magazine and contributed a sort of garden column (very loosely) for many years.

The Golowan Festival that I was involved in, as a boat owner, from the very first in 1991 is a Celtic celebration of midsummer, the Feast of John on the 24th June. From 1614 until 1934 St. Johns head on a platter was the Penzance Patron Saint, and images of it can still be seen around the town. Golowan means The Feast of John in the Cornish language.

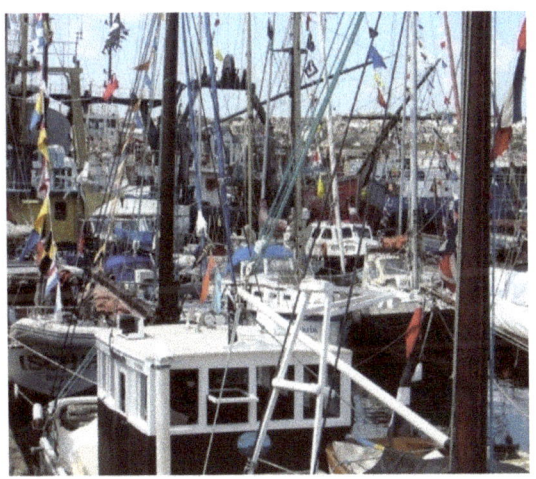 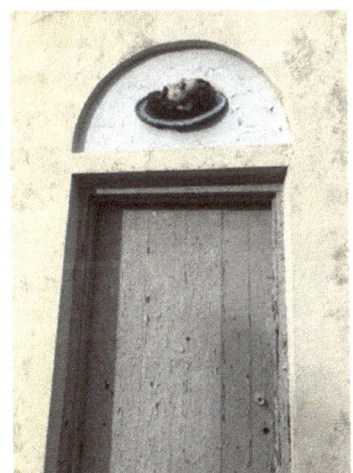 I worked mainly with Sea and Sail inviting vessels from as far as Russia to take part in the festival. The head appears in one of the paintings to show that the vessel is in Penzance as part of the festival.

The first one had tight rope artists performing across the harbour gate with members of the Dive Club swimming around below dressed as sharks. Health and Safety weren't very keen so it didn't happen again! Many of the craft in the paintings attended the festival.

When Anne's health failed I had to cut down the work load drastically and the kids bought me two canvases and said "that'll give you something to do!" A painting of Penberth Cove and Rosewall Hill, Towednack, followed and we were off! Mind to canvas – every picture tells a story.

I had a private show at the Penzance Arts Club and many of my paintings were shown at Martin Val Bakers Rainyday Gallery in Penzance. Later I was invited to join the British Naive Artists and exhibited all over the country with them.

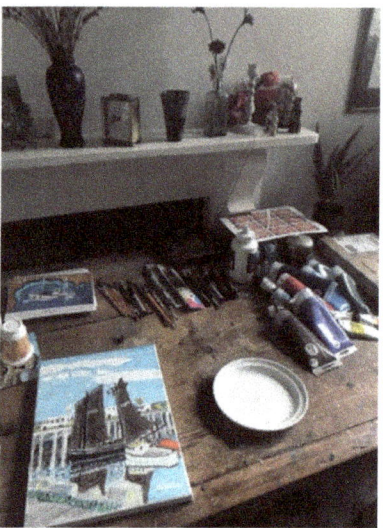

Where the magic happened!

"His colourful, cheerful works are a manifestation of his freedom to paint from life as he sees it. His paintings are warm, witty and well worth seeing."

Review from Association of British Naive Artists 2016 exhibition

N.B., All paintings in this book are Acrylics on 10x14 inches canvases, unless otherwise stated beside the pictures.

Abbey Basin

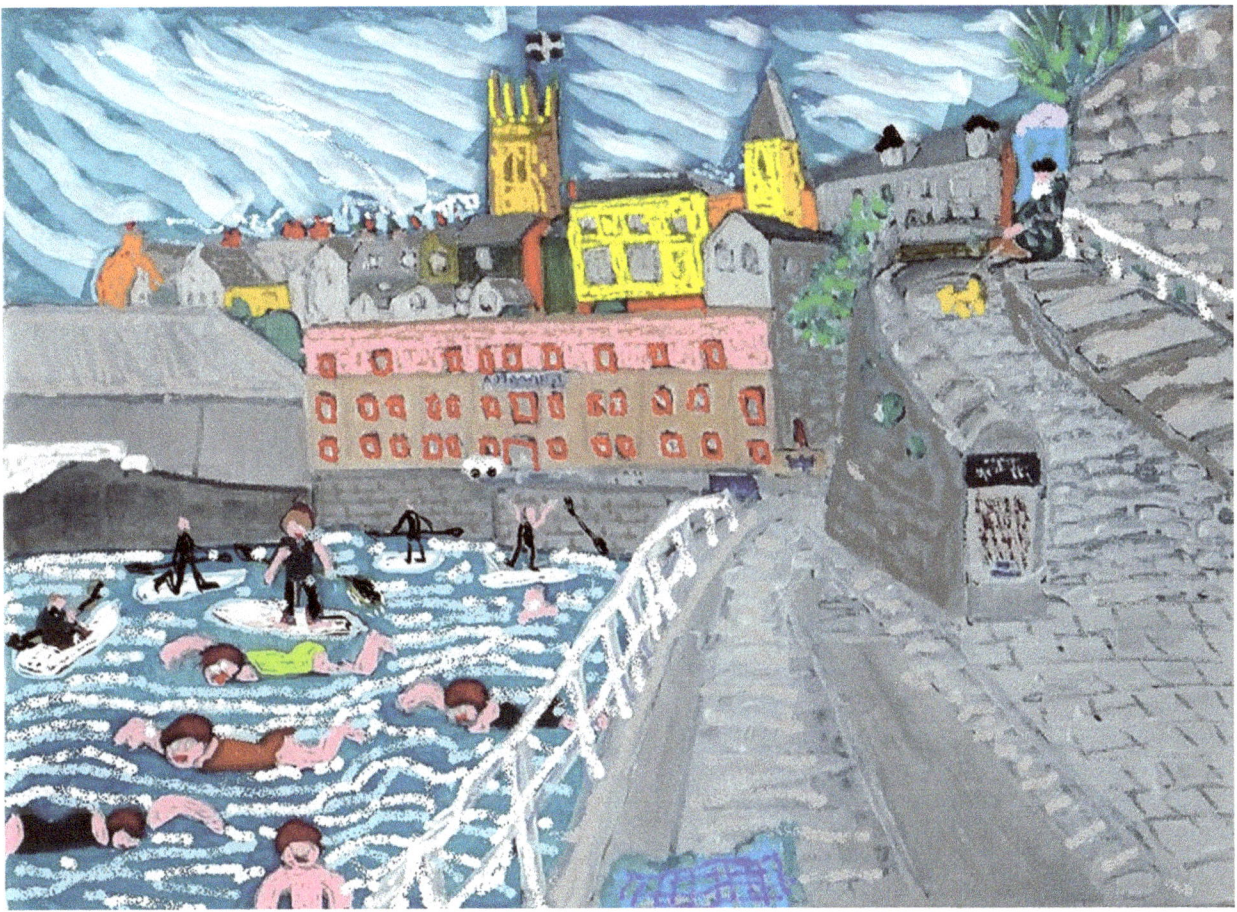

Quays and slipway. Circa early-mid C19. Dressed granite quays on the north, west and south side of Abbey Basin, with slipway and granite bollards on the west side. The later causeway and the 1881 Ross Swing Bridge, rebuilt in 1981, on the east side of Abbey Basin are not included. The 1900 dry dock on the south side and Abbey Warehouse on the west side are separately included. Part of an unusually complete group of harbour structures in Penzance.

Now used as a swimming area and for teaching stand up paddle boarding. The picture depicts the Sea Dogs, a self-help cold swimming group, and a SUP training session.

Asgaard 11

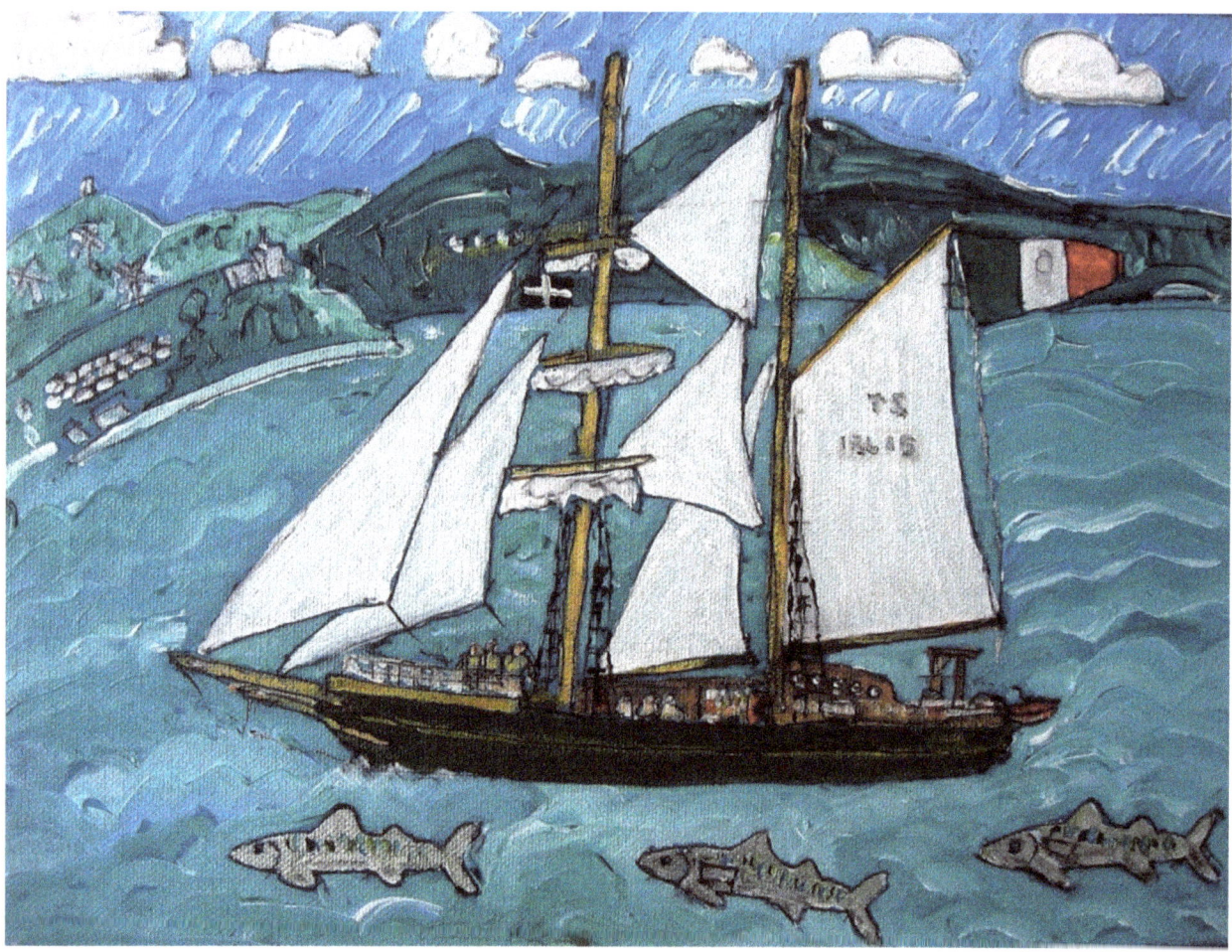

ASGAARD II - sank in the Bay of Biscay on 11 September 2008, 20 nautical miles (37 km) southwest of Belle-Île-en-Mer, at 47°18′03″N 3°33′02″W. The five crew and twenty trainees had earlier abandoned the vessel after she started taking on water. Asgaard II was heading from Falmouth to La Rochelle.

Astrid

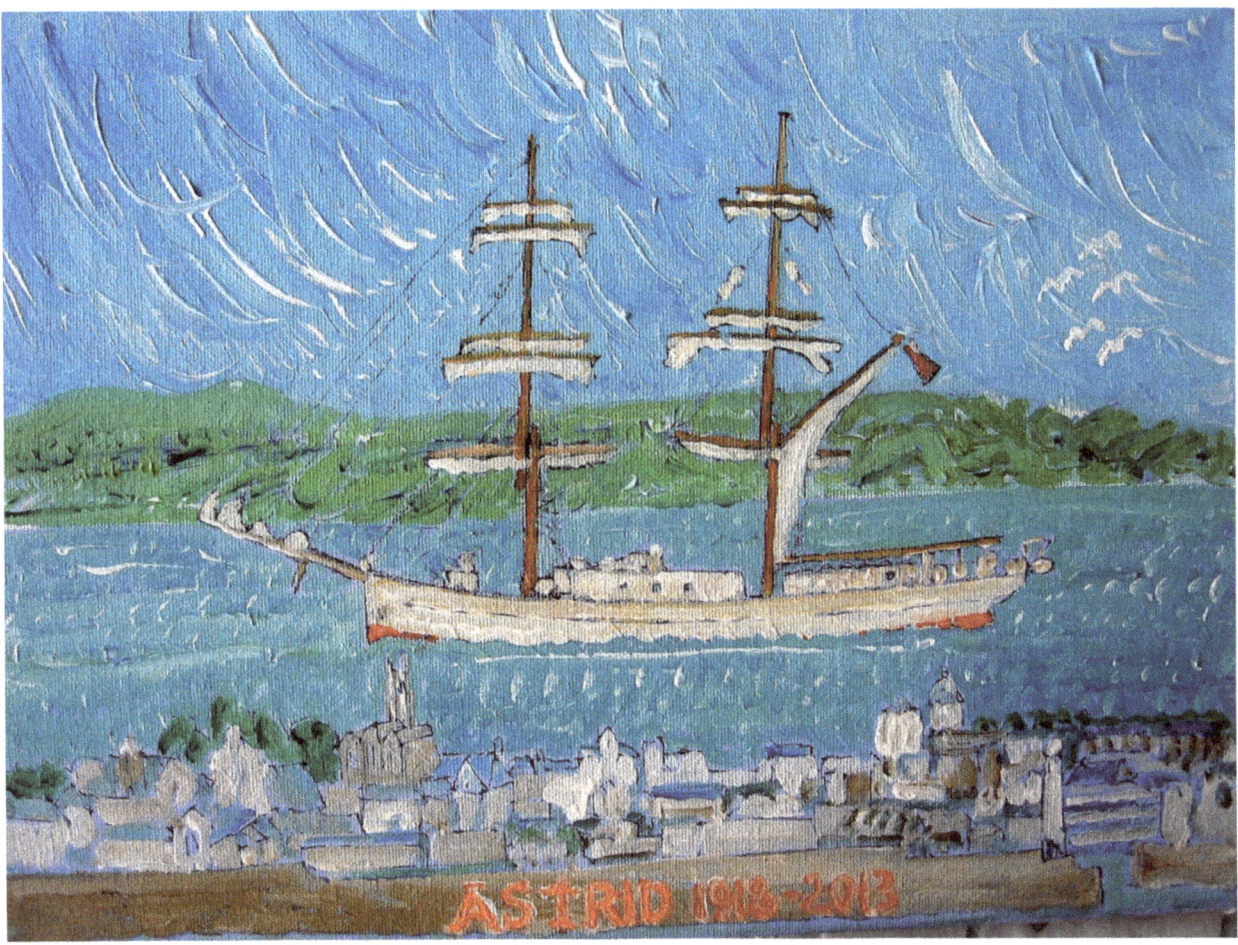

ASTRID - TV Astrid was a 41.90-metre long tall ship that was built in 1918 in the Netherlands as a lugger and originally named W.U.T.A., short for Wacht Uw Tijd Af meaning "Bide Your Time". She was later transferred to Swedish ownership, renamed Astrid and sailed on the Baltic Sea until 1975. She then sailed under a Lebanese flag and was allegedly used for drug smuggling.

Barnabas

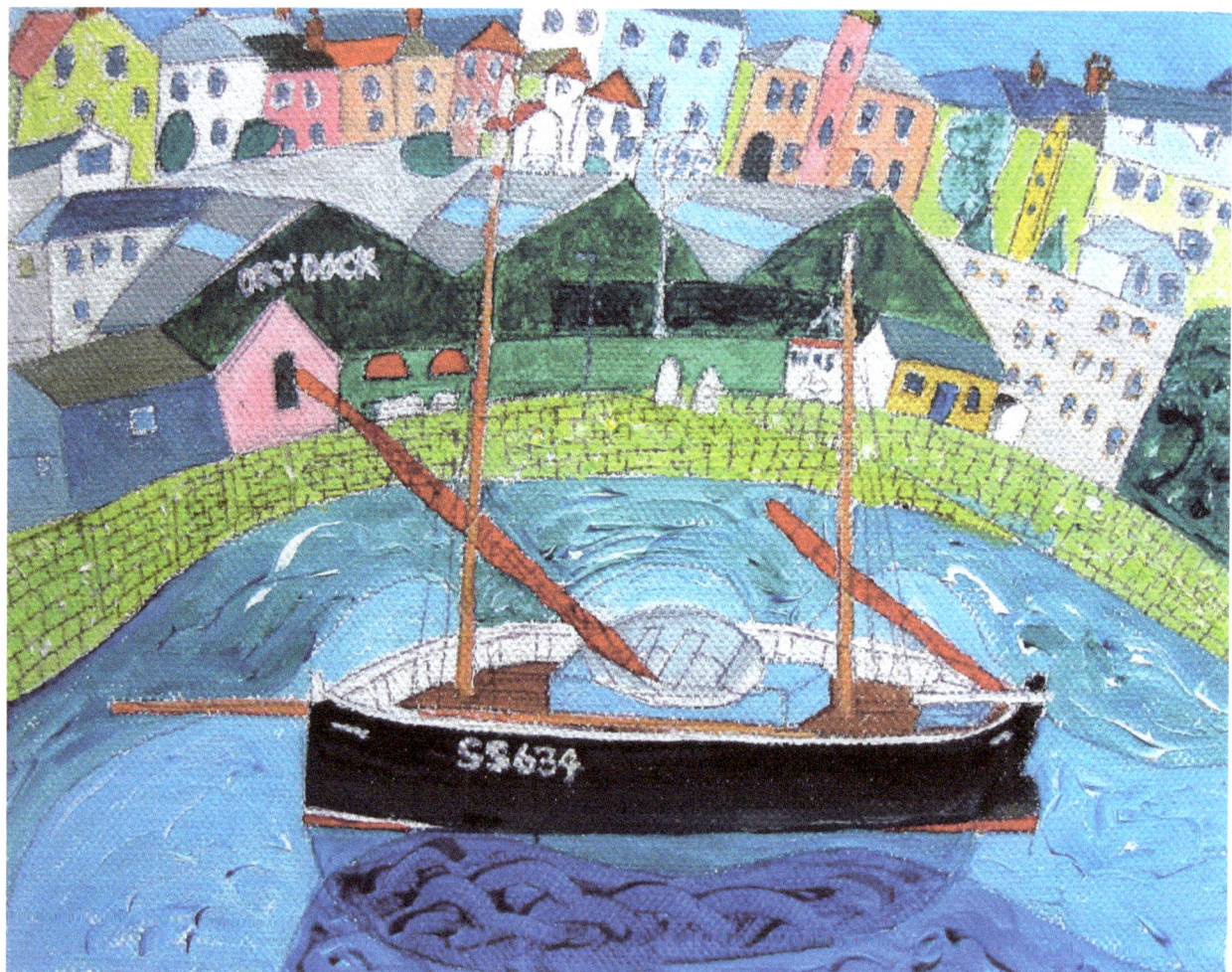

BARNABAS - is the only survivor from St Ives of the thousand-strong fleet of lug rigged seine and drift net fishing boats registered at Cornish ports at the end of the 19th century. She was built for Barnabas Thomas by Henry Trevorrow above Porthgwidden beach, St.Ives.

Barnabas was first registered on 28th October 1881 as a Class 2 pilchard boat, with the number 634 SS. Later, she was re-registered as a Class 1 mackerel driver and her number switched to SS 634. The number is said to have been chosen as it corresponded to the hymn "Will Your Anchor Hold" in the Methodist hymn book used at the time.

Bessie Ellen & Pellew

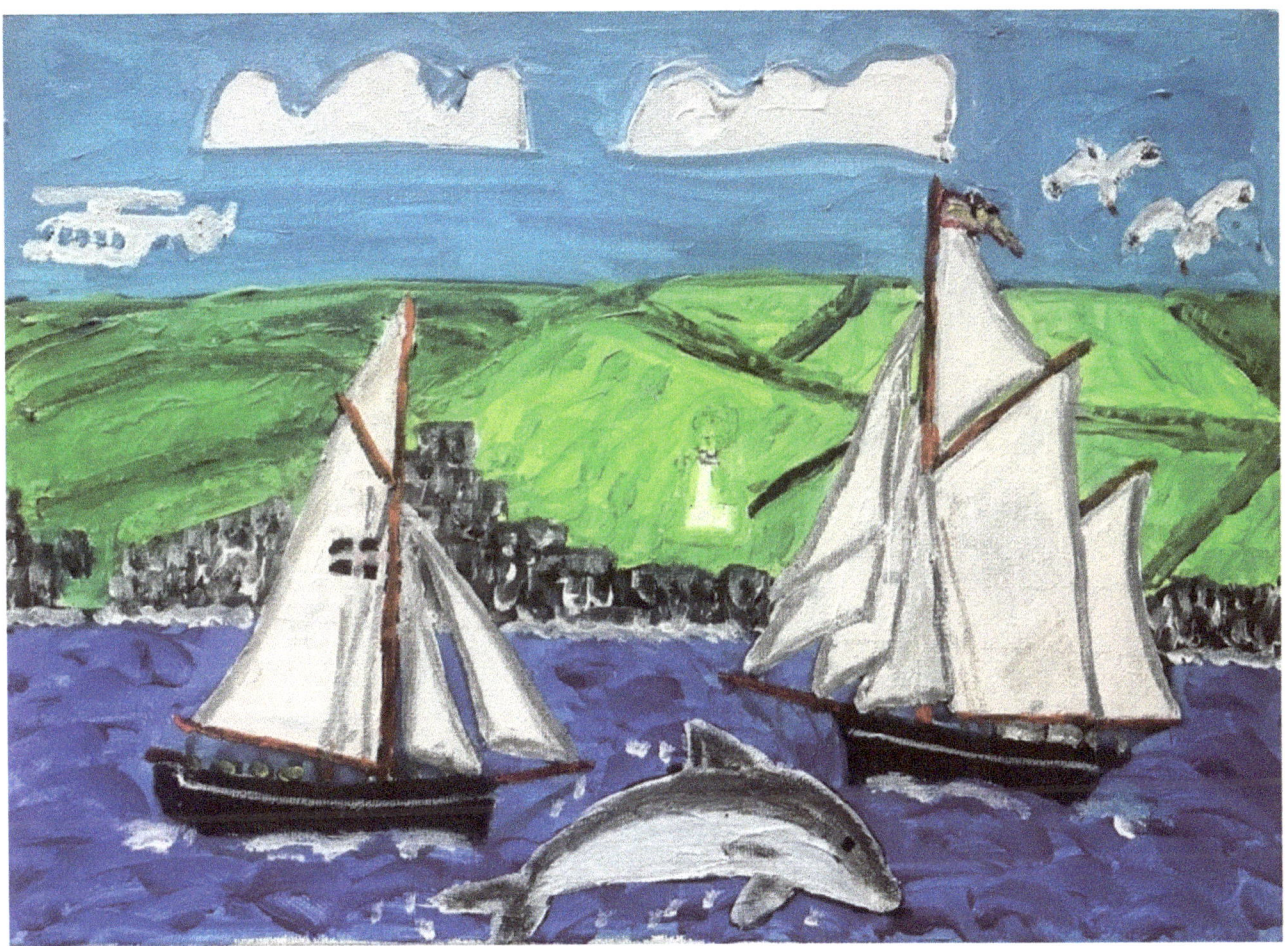

PELLEW - is a faithful recreation of the Falmouth Pilot Cutter *Vincent,* originally built in 1852 and based in St Mawes she was a familiar sight on the Fal estuary for 70 years, eventually retiring from service in 1922. Today, the spirit of tradition lives on and Pellew is strongly built to sail the oceans of the world with her guests travelling in utmost comfort and safety.

Bessie Ellen

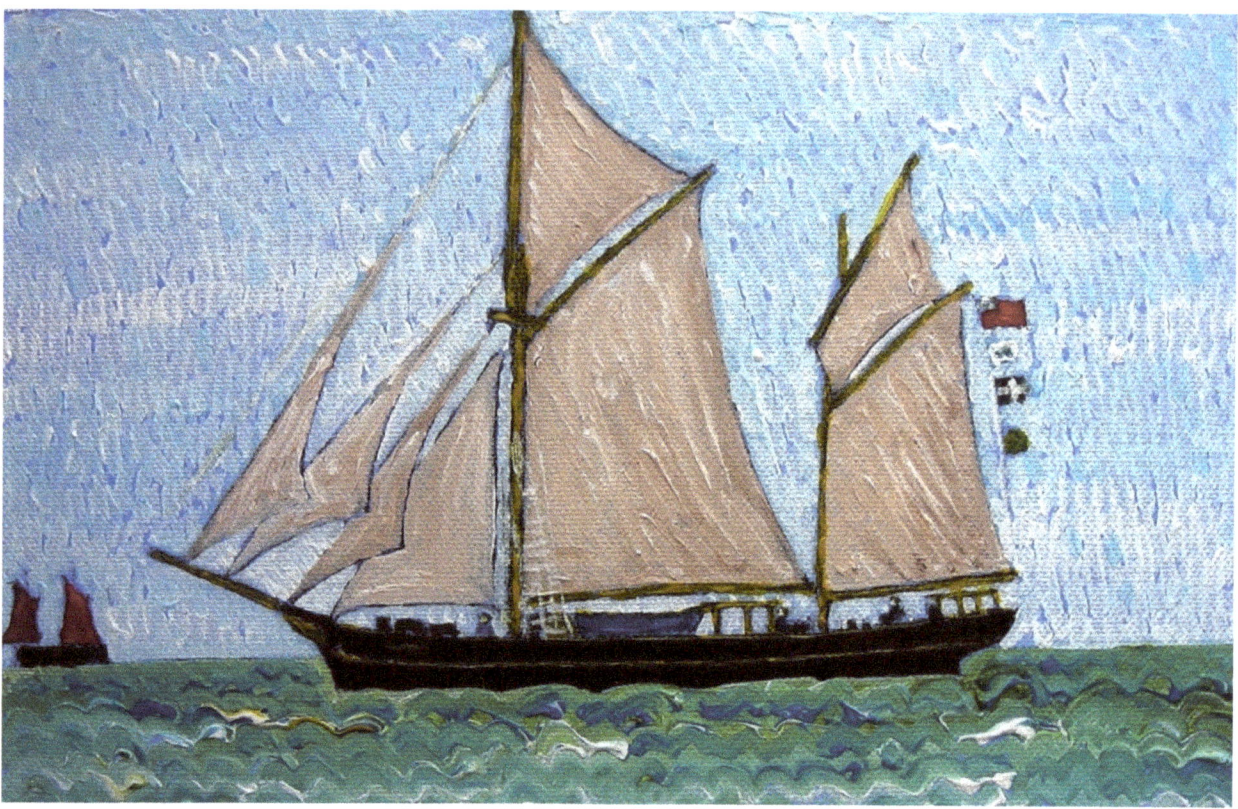

BESSIE ELLEN - Built in Plymouth, Devon, in 1904 by William Kelly, Bessie Ellen is one of the last surviving West Country trading ketches from a fleet that once stood at nearly 700. Bessie Ellen lived through an era when working sailing ships were an everyday sight in English ports and harbours.

Blue Clipper

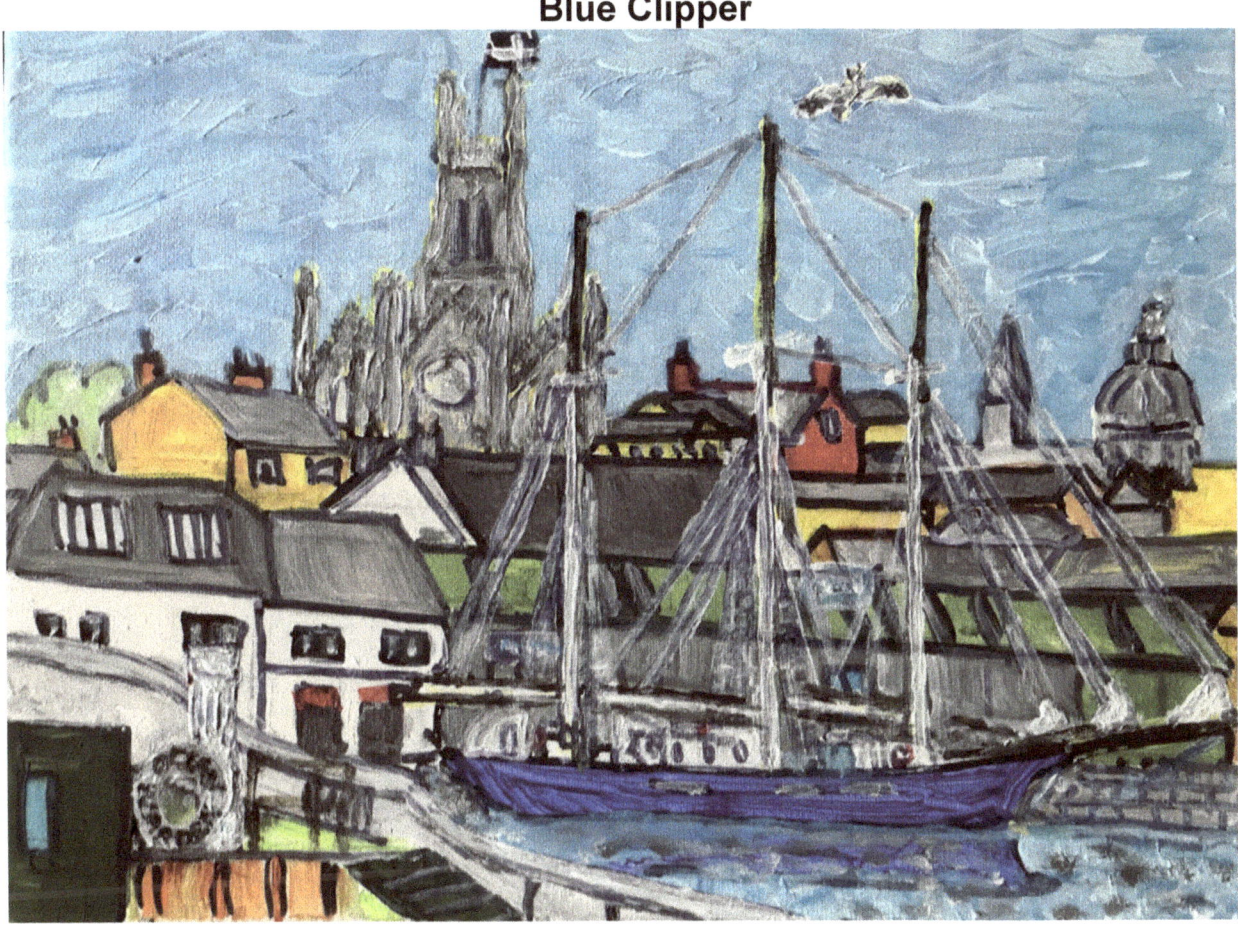

BLUE CLIPPER - Tall Ship Blue Clipper 38 meters long was built in 1991 at Feab Marstrandsverken in Sweden. In 1992 the famous brandy company Hennessey chartered Blue Clipper to celebrate the anniversary of the first delivery of cognac from France to Shanghai 120 years earlier. Painted white and with the name 'Spirit of Hennessey' Blue Clipper repeated this historic voyage. She has appeared in various TV programmes and TV commercials including the Trade Winds TV series starring Hugh Johnson. Following this, she went into private ownership and sailed in Mediterranean waters under a Maltese flag. Maybe Sailing acquired the ship in 2016. After an extensive maintenance period the ship sailed to London to begin a 5 month tall ship Regatta, the 2017 Rendez-Vous. The ship was one of only four vessels to complete the whole race, travelling over 10,000 nautical miles visiting Portugal, the Canaries, Bermuda, USA, Canada and France. This Regatta was to commemorate the 150th Anniversary of the Canadian Federation. It was an extremely successful regatta for Blue Clipper and her crew, placing either 1st or 2nd in four of the five race legs. 2018 marked a new chapter for the vessel, as she was repainted Blue and travelled north once more to visit the Arctic before heading to the Caribbean for some winter sunshine.

Breton Crabber

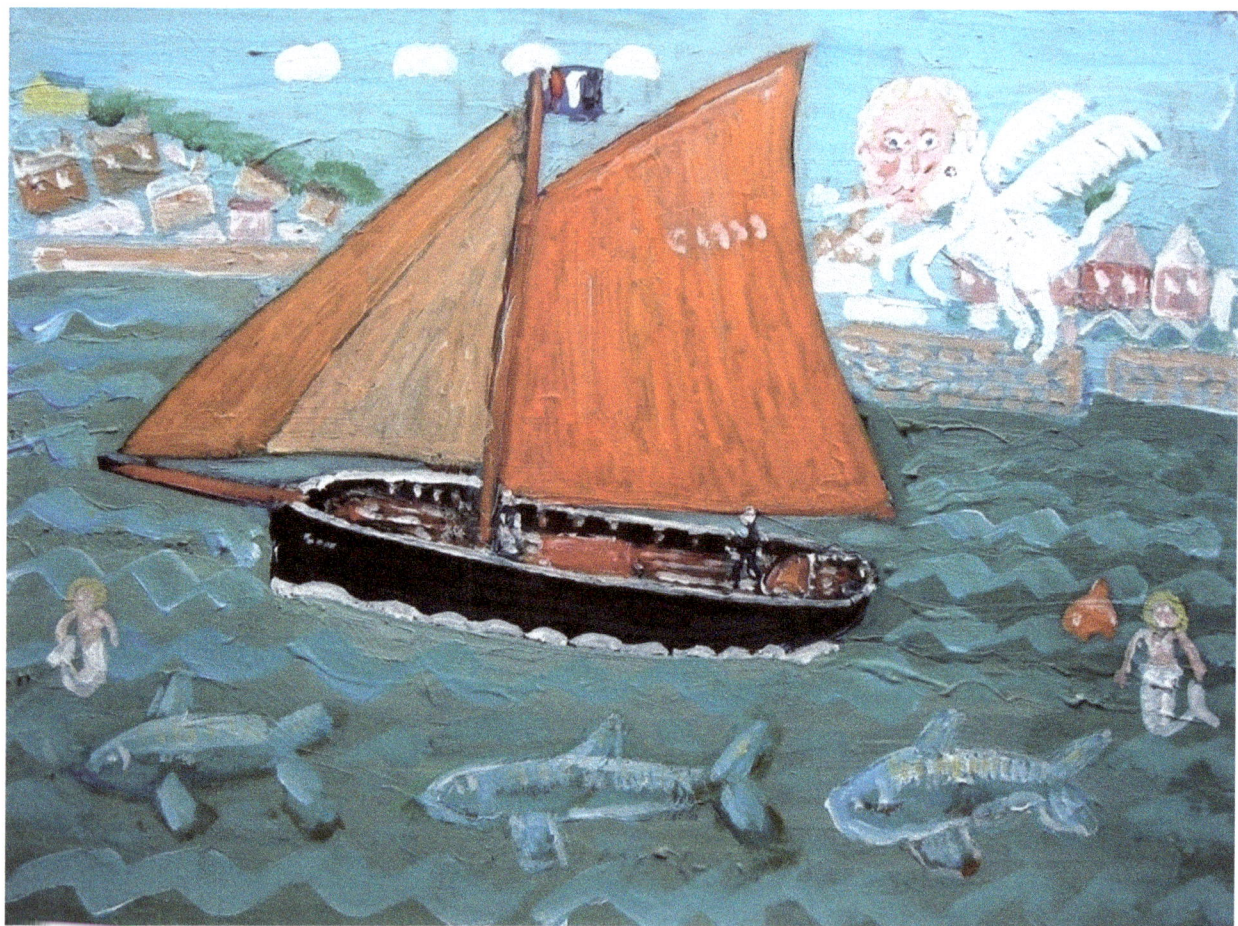

BRETON CRABBERS - All the Breton crabbers were well-built, and far better-built than the French wooden trawlers of that day. Boats of the style that the Pen Glas is are simply first class as far as the build is concerned, and I'm told they are excellent in sea keeping. Known to many as 'Camaret boats', they were built at places like Douarnenez, Audierne and Camaret itself; and I don't care what anyone says, as far as construction is concerned, the potters of that style beat the French wooden trawlers hands-down.

Captain Ahab

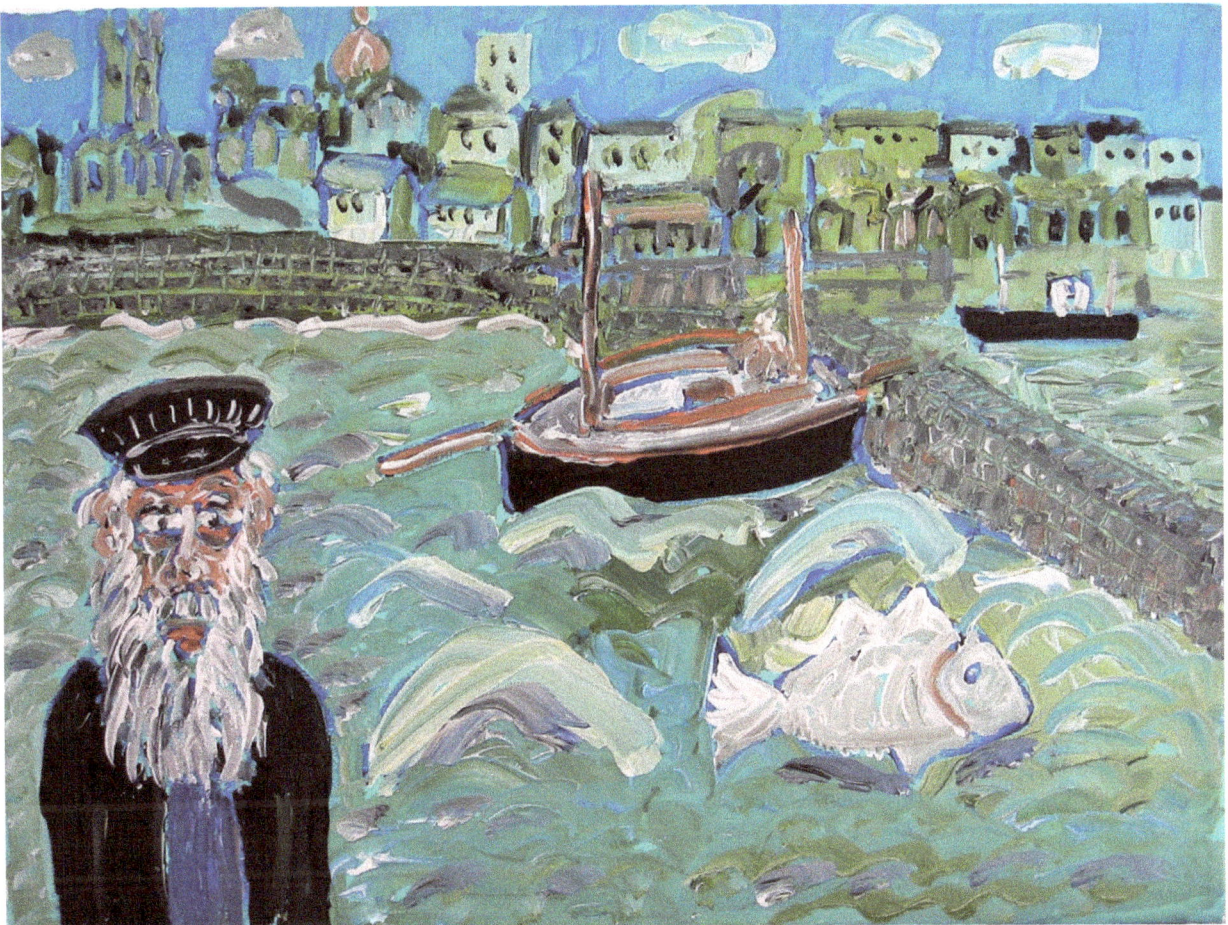

Ahab waiting for the ferry

CAPTAIN AHAB - The fictional character of Captain Ahab, a one-legged captain of the whaling vessel Pequod in the novel Moby Dick -LRB- 1851 -RRB-, by Herman Melville. Find out how his obsession with killing the whale causes his own death and those of his crew members, and how it is interpreted by various perspectives.

Carlos de Amesquita

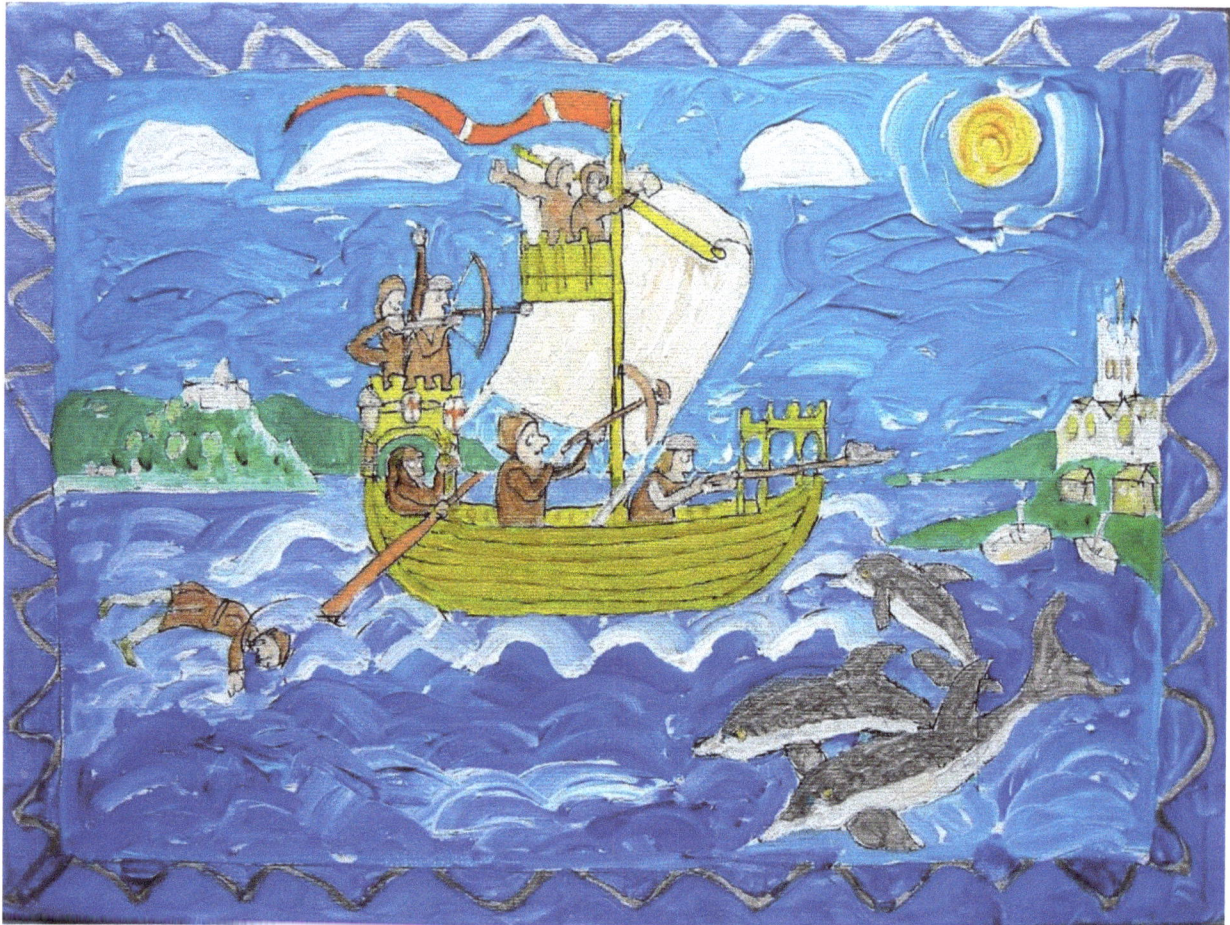

Approaching the Dock Inn with apprehension

CARLOS DE AMÉSQUITA (also Carlos de Amézqueta or Carlos de Amézola) was a Spanish naval officer of the 16th century. He is remembered for his raid on English soil, known as the Raid on Mount's Bay, in the context of the Brittany Campaign during the Anglo-Spanish War 1585–1604. Amésquita commanded three companies and four galleys (named Capitana, Patrona, Peregrina and Bazana). They disembarked at Penmarch on July 26, and in Mount's Bay (Cornwall) on August 2. After burning the town of Mousehole, Amésquita and his men embarked on their galleys and sailed for two miles, after which they disembarked again, conquered and burned the fort f Penzance down, Newlyn, and Penzance. They celebrated a mass at St. Mary Chapel at Penzance, where they promised to celebrate another mass after England had been defeated.

Corydalis

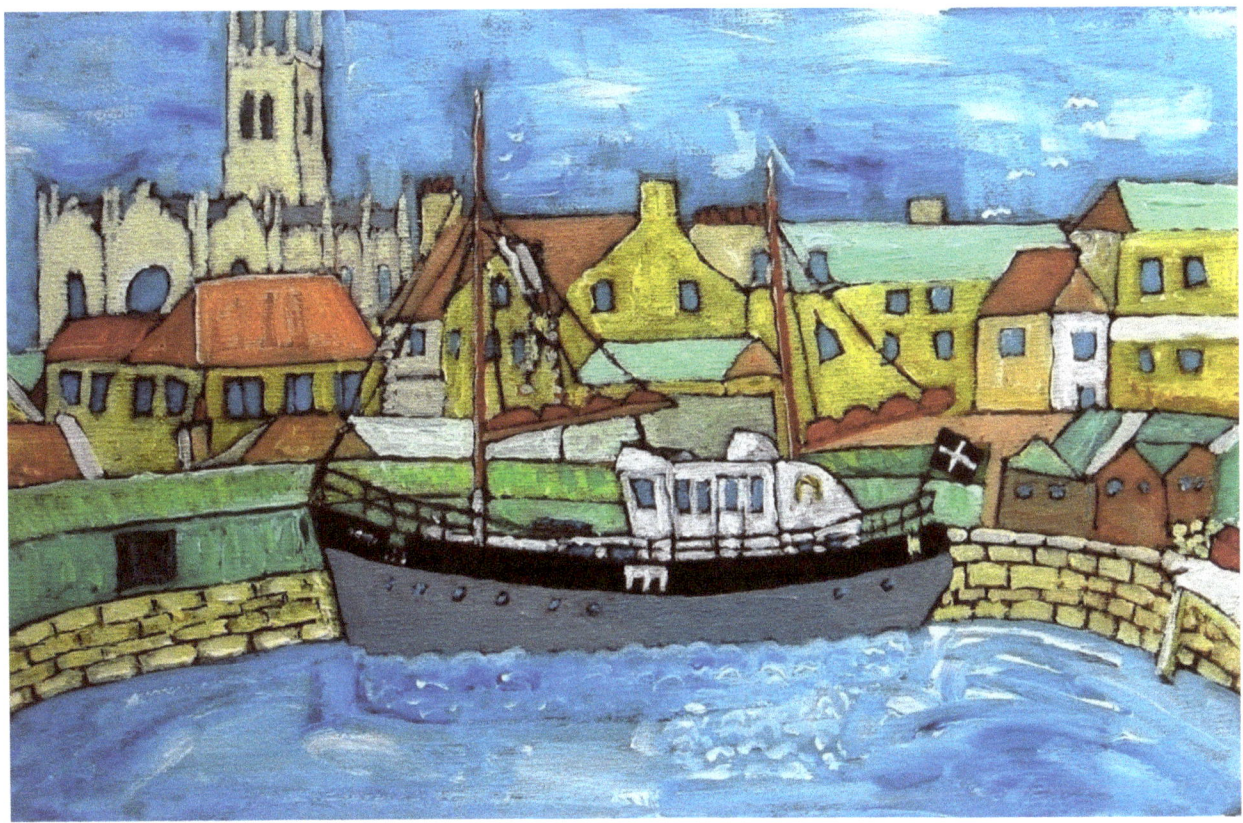

CORYDALIS - is a 'one off' Trawler Motor Vessel Gaff Rigged Ketch. Designed by Stuart Platt and his wife Baroness Beryl Platt of Winch Essex and built by the renowned boat builder Derrick Hythe of Plymouth in 1989.

Courier

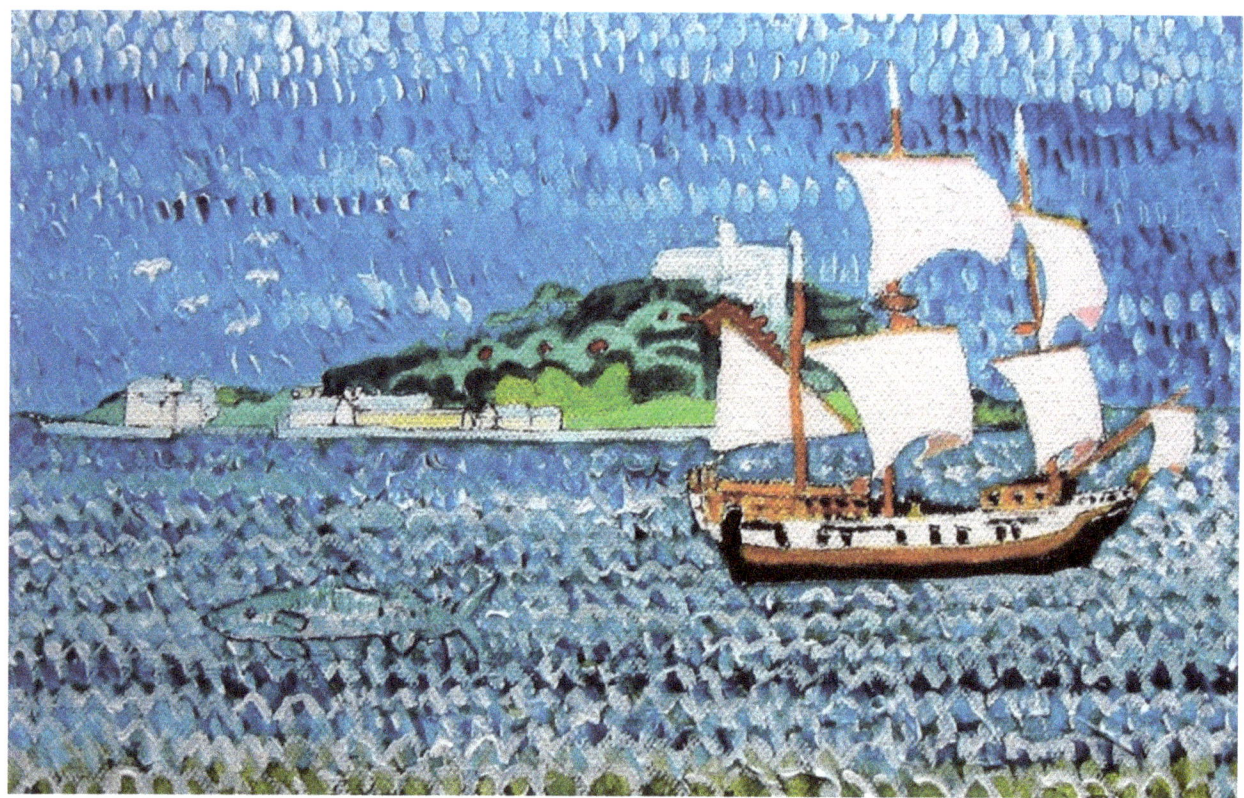

COURIER - Sailed from Kaliningrad, Russia, to be at the Golowan Festival, Sea and Sail in Penzance. Courier was a replica of corvette Courier of 1703. 87' x 17'6. Built in 1993. Owned by Polar Odyssey Marine Club, Petrosavodsk, Onegasee, Russia.

Crazy Diamond

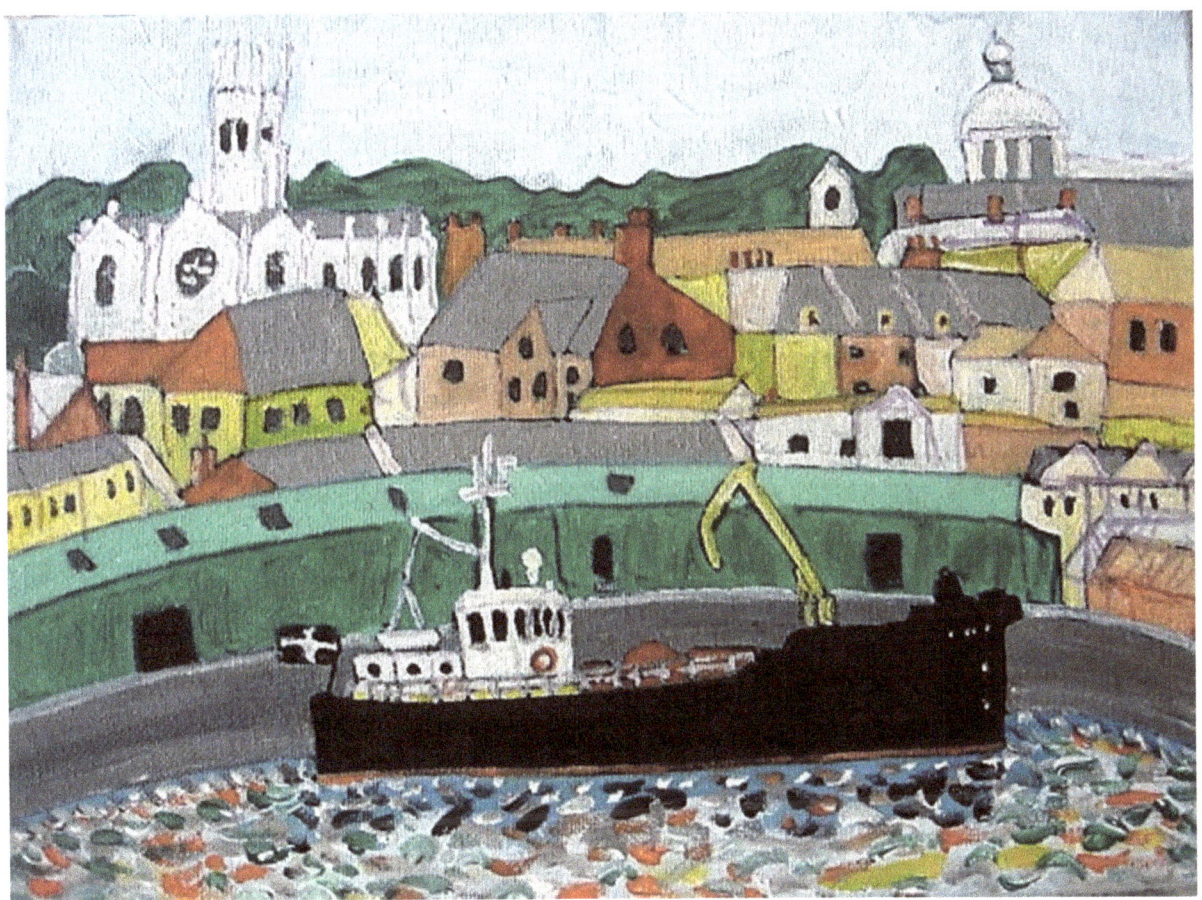

CRAZY DIAMOND - "Shine On You Crazy Diamond" is a nine-part Pink Floyd composition written by David Gilmour, Roger Waters, and Richard Wright, which appeared on Pink Floyd's 1975 concept album *Wish You Were Here*. The song is written about and dedicated to founder member Syd Barrett, who departed from the band in 1968 after becoming mentally ill.

Crazy Diamond was used to carry freight to the Isles of Scilly etc. The local owner also had two cable layers and a MTB that was based in the Norwegian fjords in order to sink Russian nuclear submarines in the event of war.

De Gallant

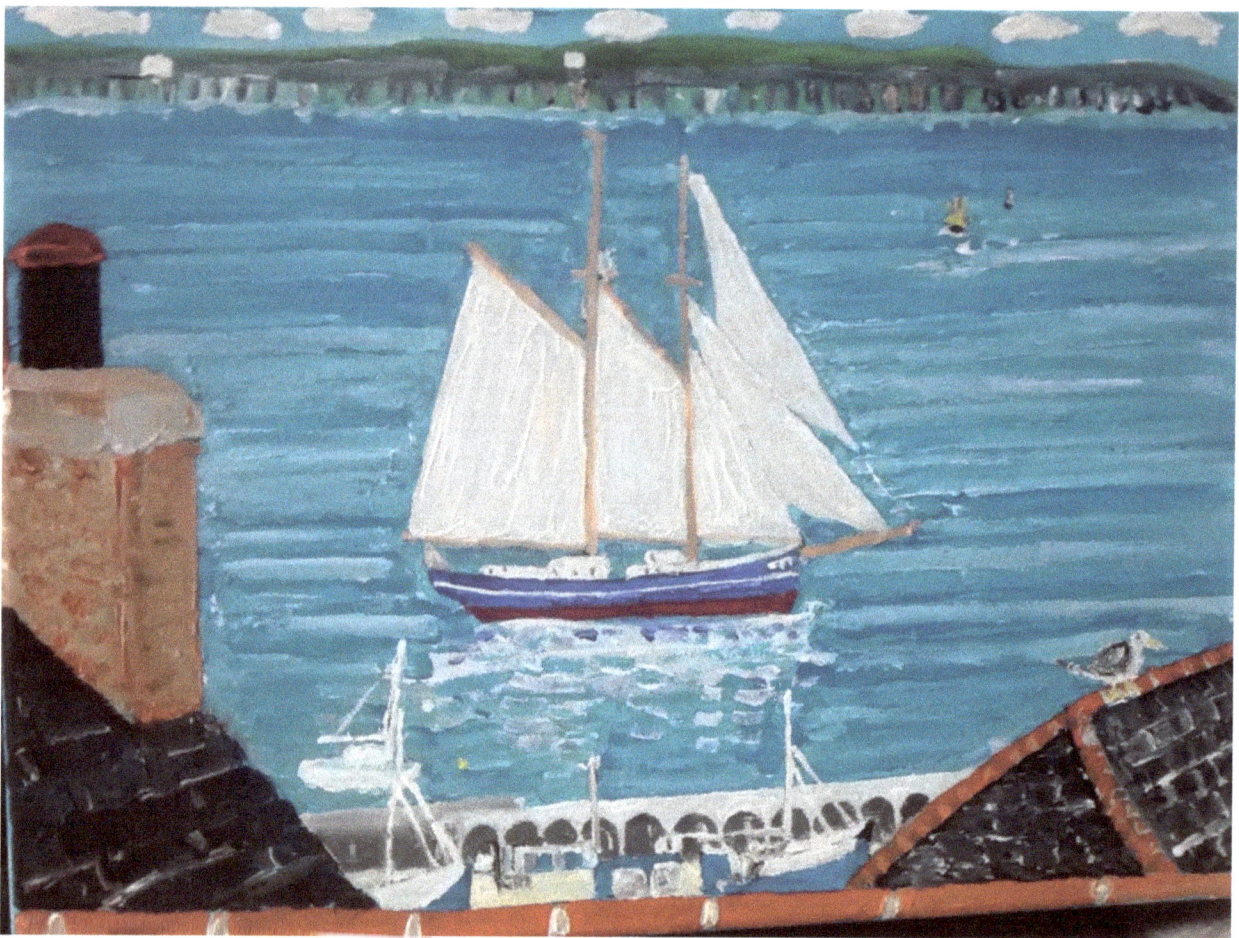

DE GALLANT, built in Vlaardingen, the Netherlands, in the yard of the Figee brothers and launched in 1916 under the name Jannetje Margaretha. De Gallant sank on the 21st May 2024. She encountered an unexpected and violent storm off Great Inagua, the southernmost island in the Bahamas, carrying cargo to Europe from Columbia.

Dragon Fly

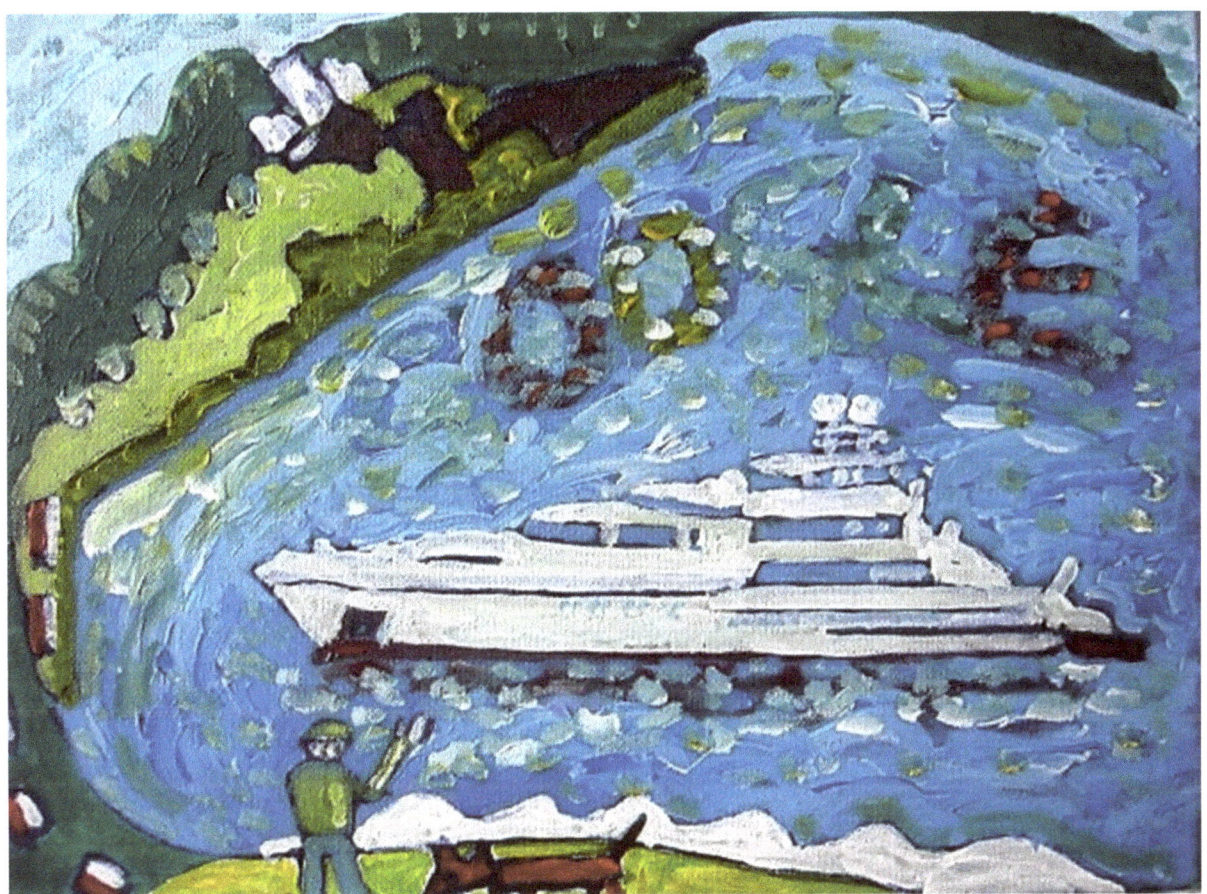

Dragon Fly-Sergy Brin

DRAGON FLY - Brin is the owner of the yacht **Dragonfly**. The Dragonfly yacht, originally known as Silver Zwei, was constructed by Silver Yachts and later purchased by Sergej **Brin**. The yacht is a luxury haven for 14 guests and a crew of 16, showcasing the exceptional design work of Espen Oeino.

Dream Boat

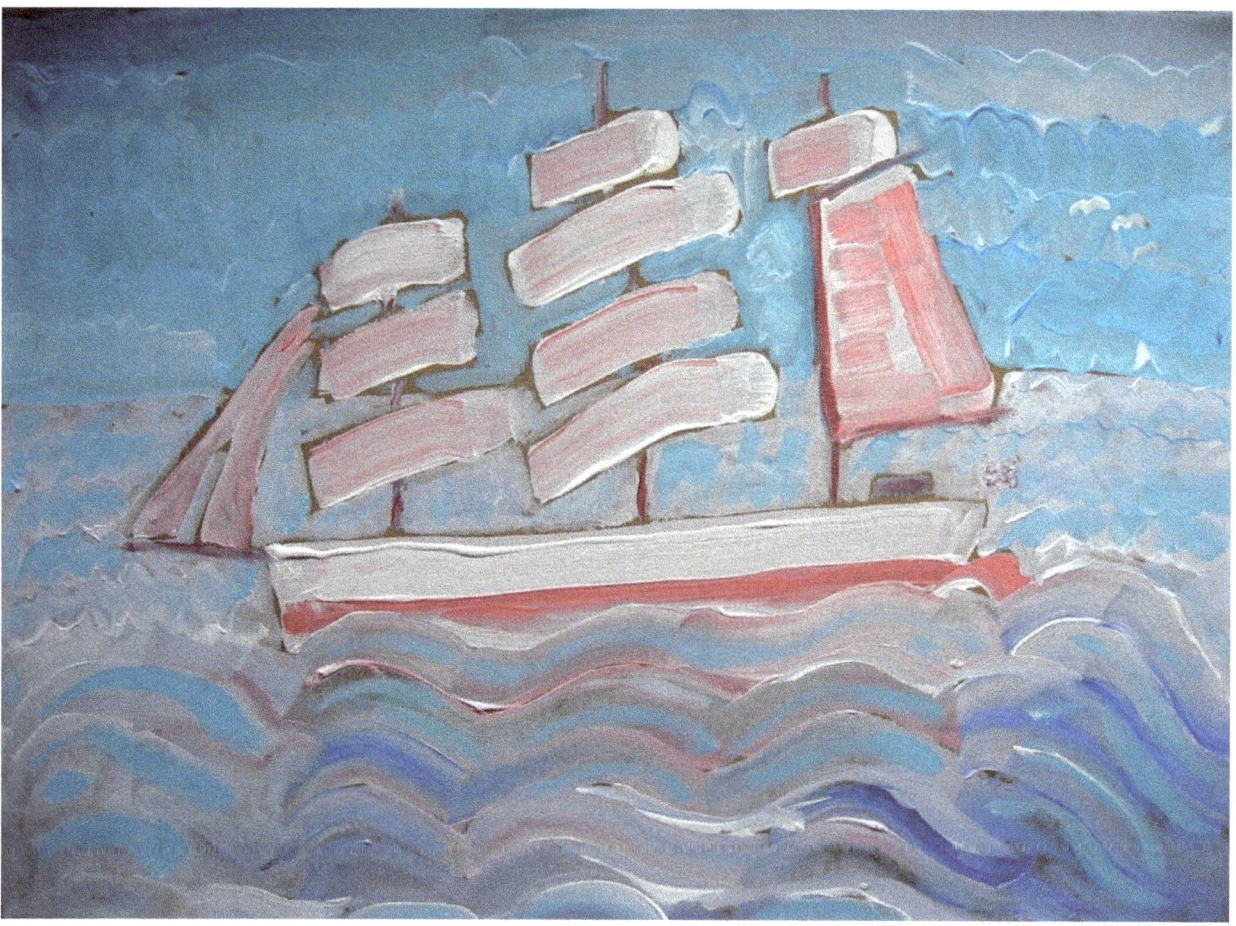

DREAM BOAT - dreamboat (n.) "Romantically desirable person" 1947, from **dream** (n.) + **boat** (n.). The phrase was in use about two decades before that. "When My **Dream Boat** Comes Home" was the title of a 1936 song credited to Guy Lombardo and "**Dream Boat**" was the title of a 1929 book.

Earl of Pembroke

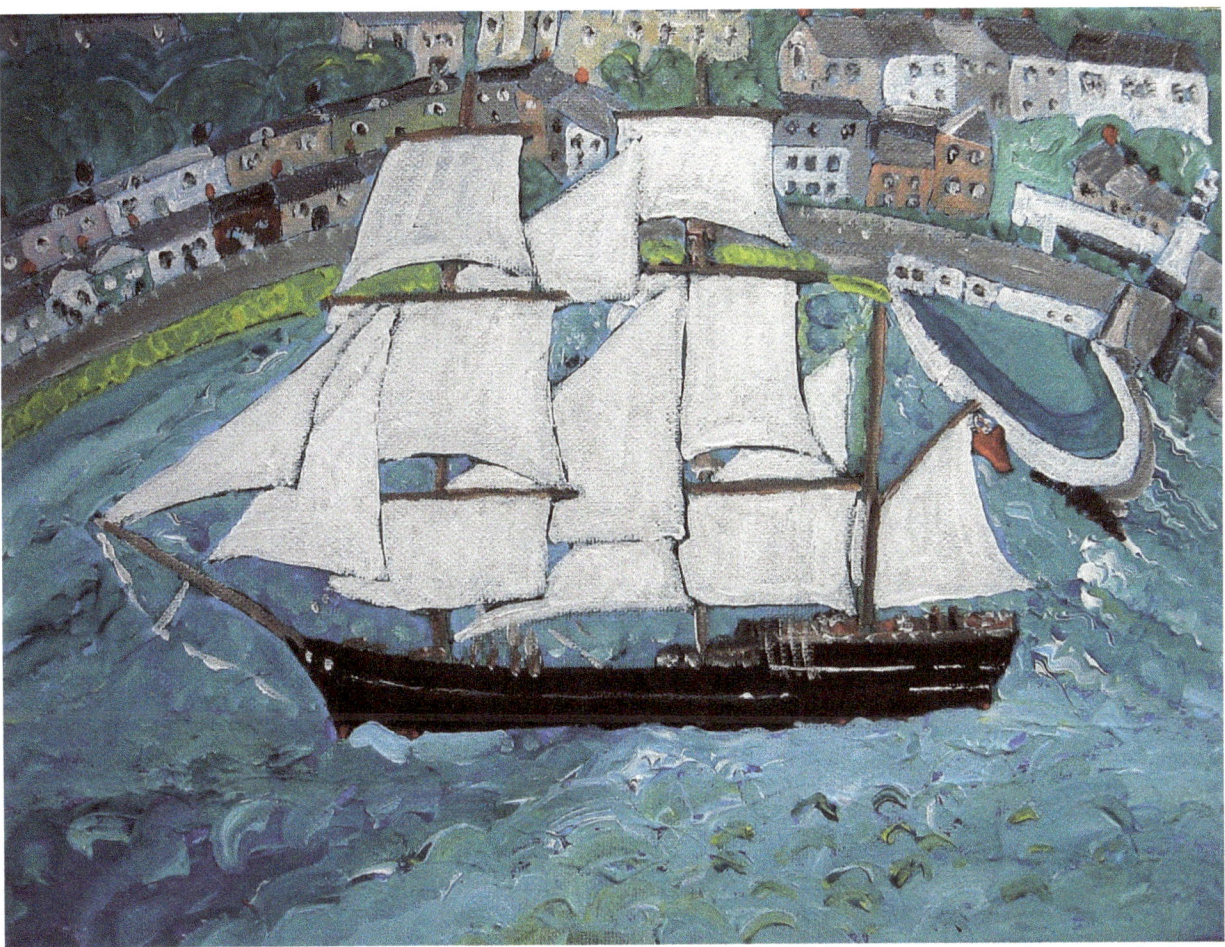

THE EARL OF PEMBROKE - was built in Sweden 1945, when she was known as Orion, and was used to haul timber in the Baltic Sea until being laid up in Denmark in 1974. The 44.2-metre ship was later moved to the UK in 1980 where full restoration work began in 1985, with film work in mind.

The restoration saw the rig changed from a schooner to a barque type, which more closely resembled Captain Cook's 'HMS Endeavour'. The vessel was scrapped in Kampen on 2 December 2022.

Elizabeth and Blanche

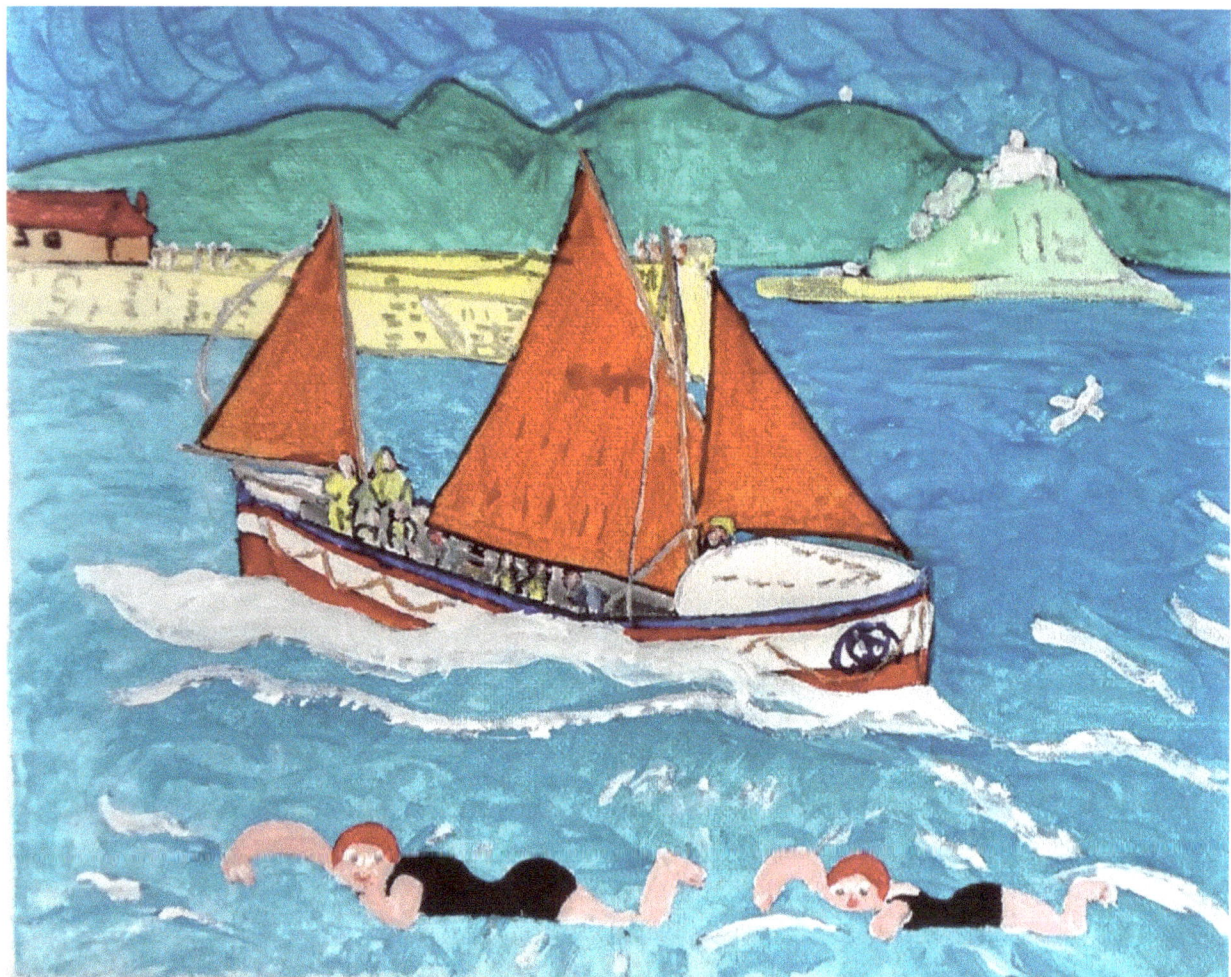

ELIZABETH AND BLANCHE II - The launching of the lifeboat 'Elizabeth and Blanche II' from Penzance Harbour. She was built in 1899 and stationed in Penzance from 1899 to 1908. In November 1907 the Thames barge, Baltic, was wrecked off Mousehole Island. Her crew was rescued by local men in the crabber, Lady White as the Elizabeth and Blanche got stuck in the mud in Penzance Harbour. In 1908 she was moved to Newlyn and kept under cover near the Old Harbour. In 1913 the Penlee Lifeboat House was inaugurated where she was kept until 1922. Her most famous service was to the Norwegian barque Saluto on 13 December 1911 when 13 crew were rescued.

Ellian

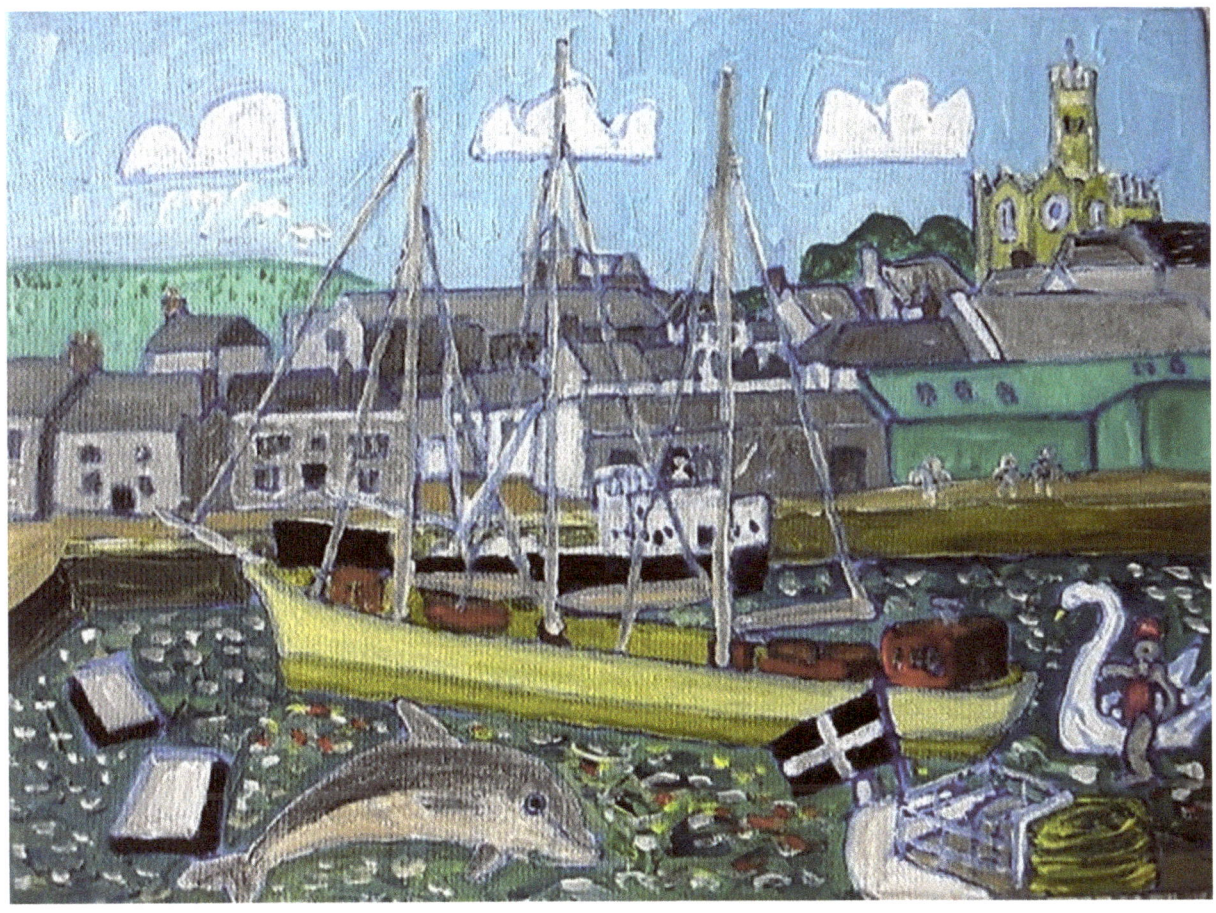

Ellian 1955

ELIAN - Last sailing vessel delivering coal from Cardiff 1955, Wales, and Elian. Involved in the coastal trade.

Roger Lowry

Evening view

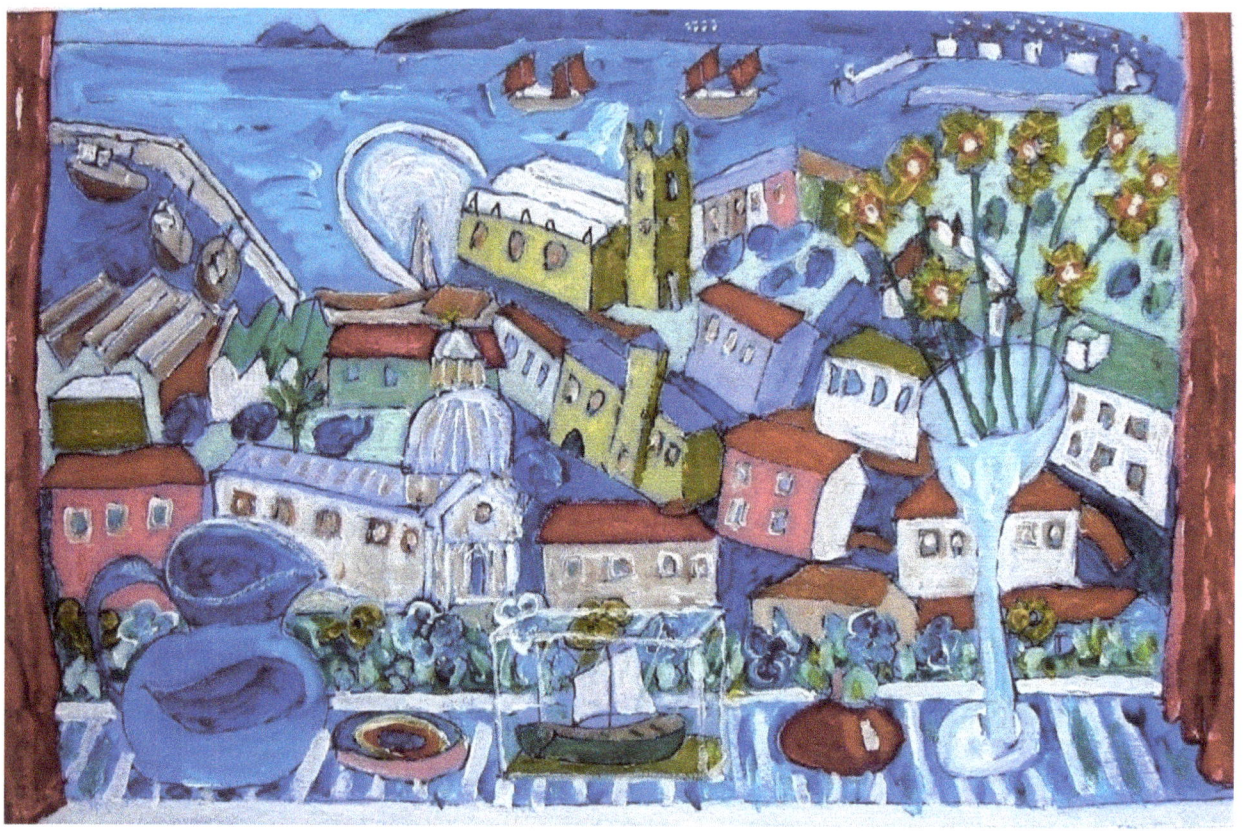

Evening view with two luggers

An imaginary view looking over Penzance from our bedroom window.

Excelsior

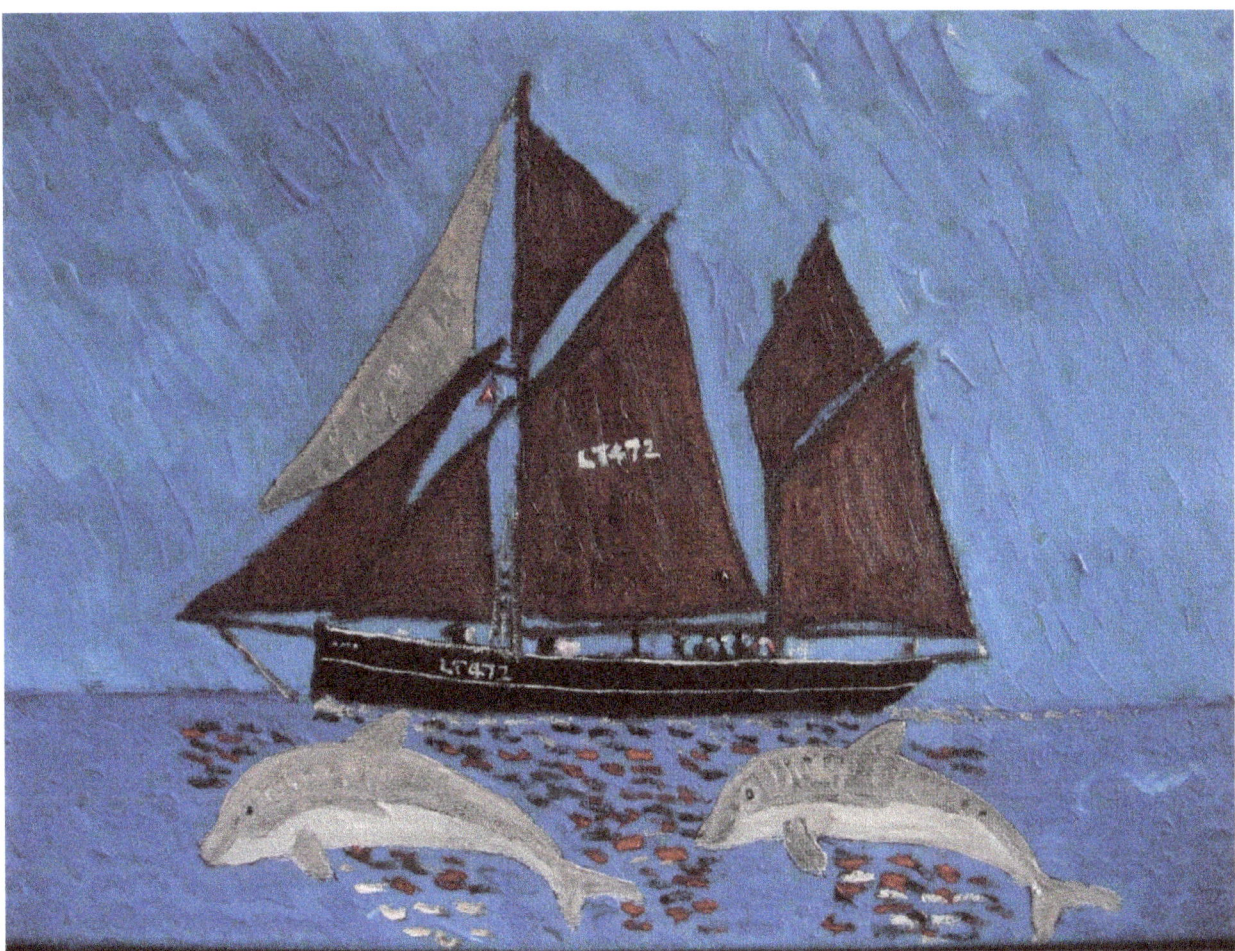

EXCELSIOR - She was built in 1921 by John Chambers & Co of Lowestoft to trawl the southern North Sea. During the Depression of the 1930s she was sold to Norway. The Norwegians converted her to a motor coaster, removing her topmast and bowsprit and installing a wheelhouse on deck. She was used to transport general cargo around the Norwegian, Swedish and Danish coasts. John Wylson heard that the owners of a motor coaster called SVINØR were retiring. He returned to Norway the following summer to see her and bought her, sailing her back to Lowestoft just over 50 years after she had been built there as EXCELSIOR LT472 in 1921!.

Eye of the Wind

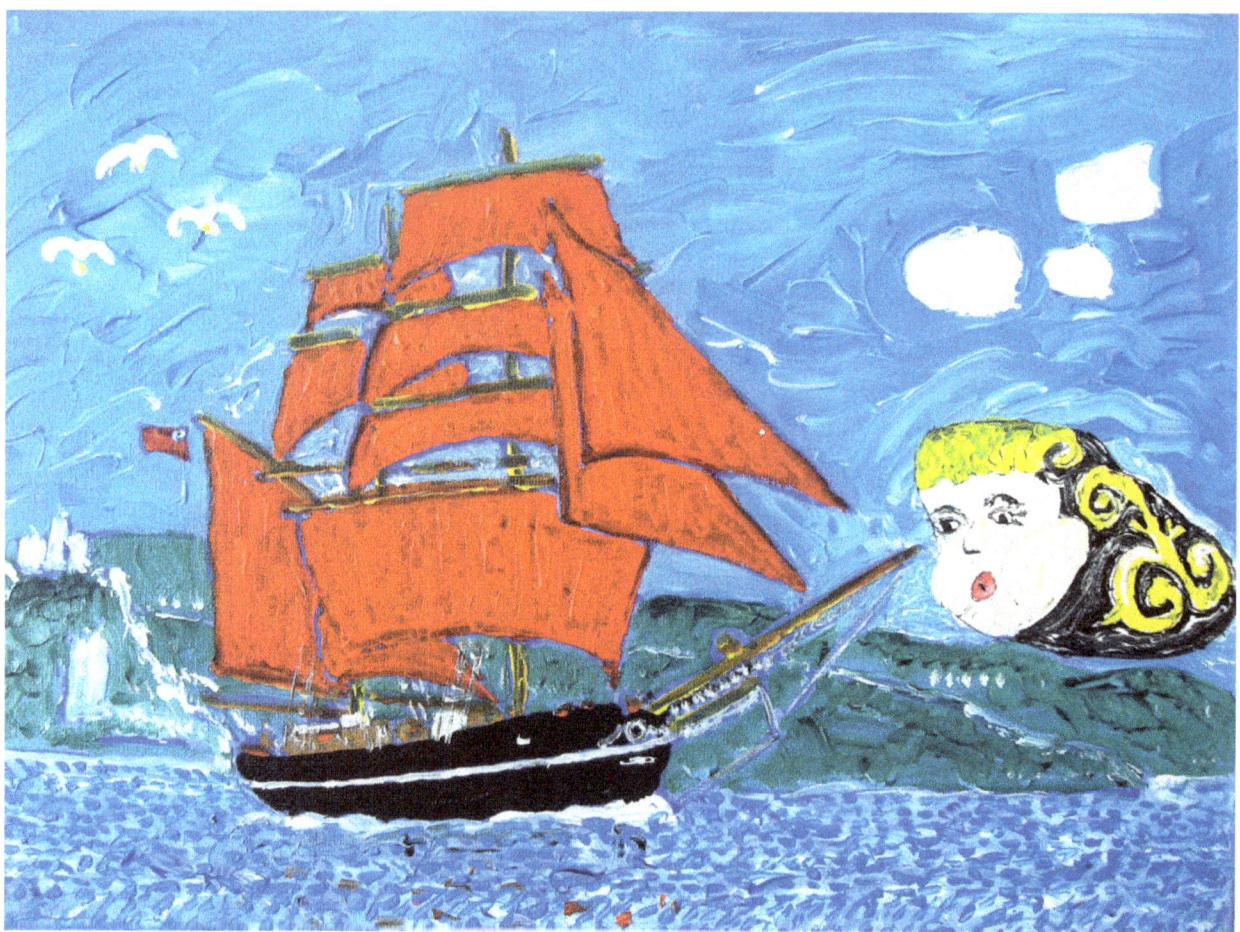

THE EYE OF THE WIND - is owned and operated by FORUM train & sail GmbH. In 1911, the Lühring shipyard at Brake/Germany built a topsail schooner, which was baptised by her owner, Captain Johann Friedrich Kolb from Fockbek near Rendsburg, with the name "Friedrich". In March 1924, the ship was sold to the ship owner Axel Ageberg in Kalmar in Sweden and was named "Sam." Only two years later she was acquired by the shipping company KH Hendriksson in Stockevik/Sweden. After a Jönköpings-two-stroke engine was fitted, she became a motor schooner and spent 30 years criss-crossing the Baltic and North Sea as a cargo ship "Merry."

Feasible

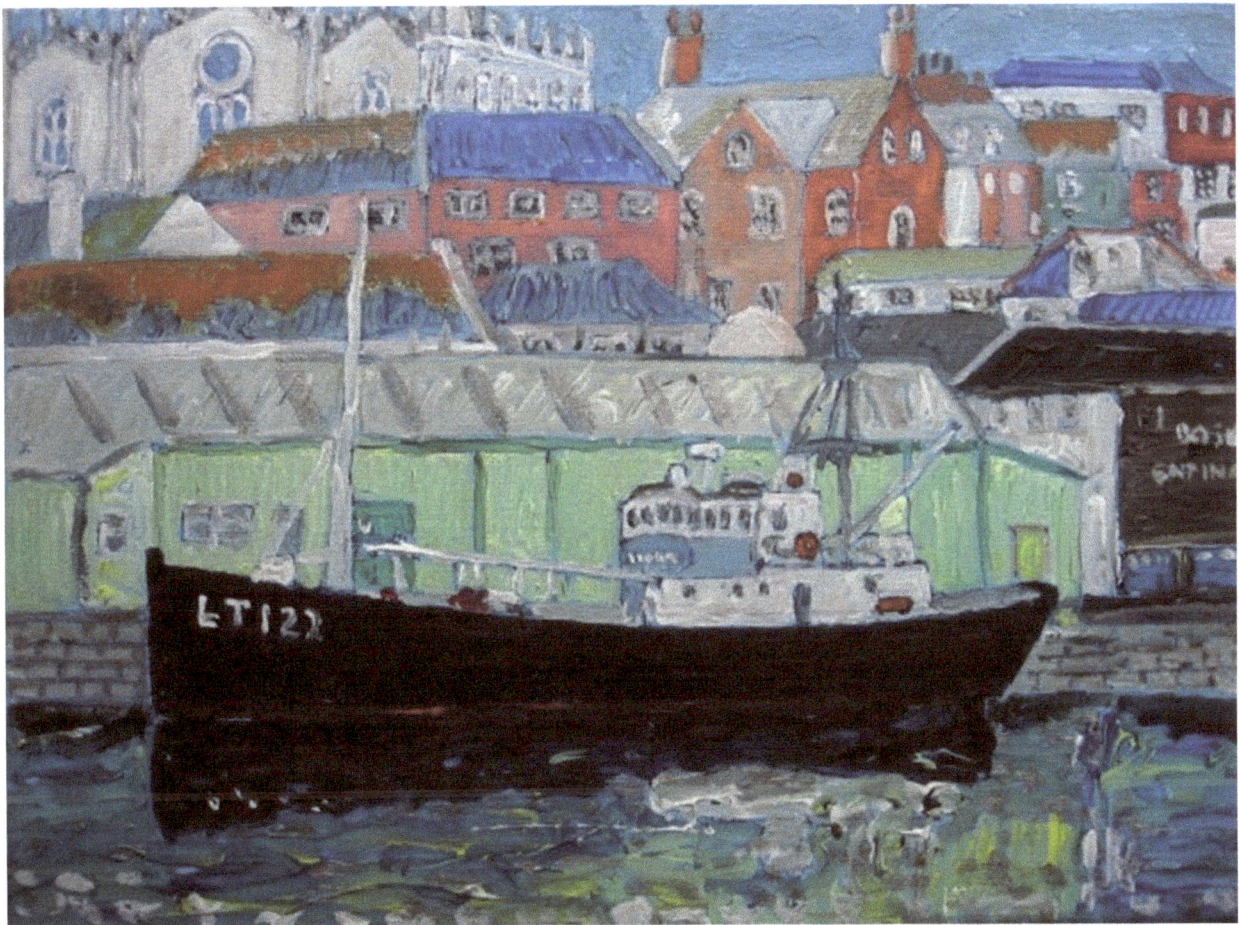

FEASIBLE - was built in 1912 by John Duthie of Aberdeen as a steam drifter and still has her original steam winches and derricks. In 2007, FEASIBLE was located in Penzance harbour having been bought by her current owner in 1997 and sailed down from the Isle of Wight. Each time an attempt was made to round Land's End with her 1903 engine, it stopped and the lifeboat had to be called. Finally, the engine was given back to its country of origin; Norway, for use in the Bruvnoll Museum.

Ghost Ship

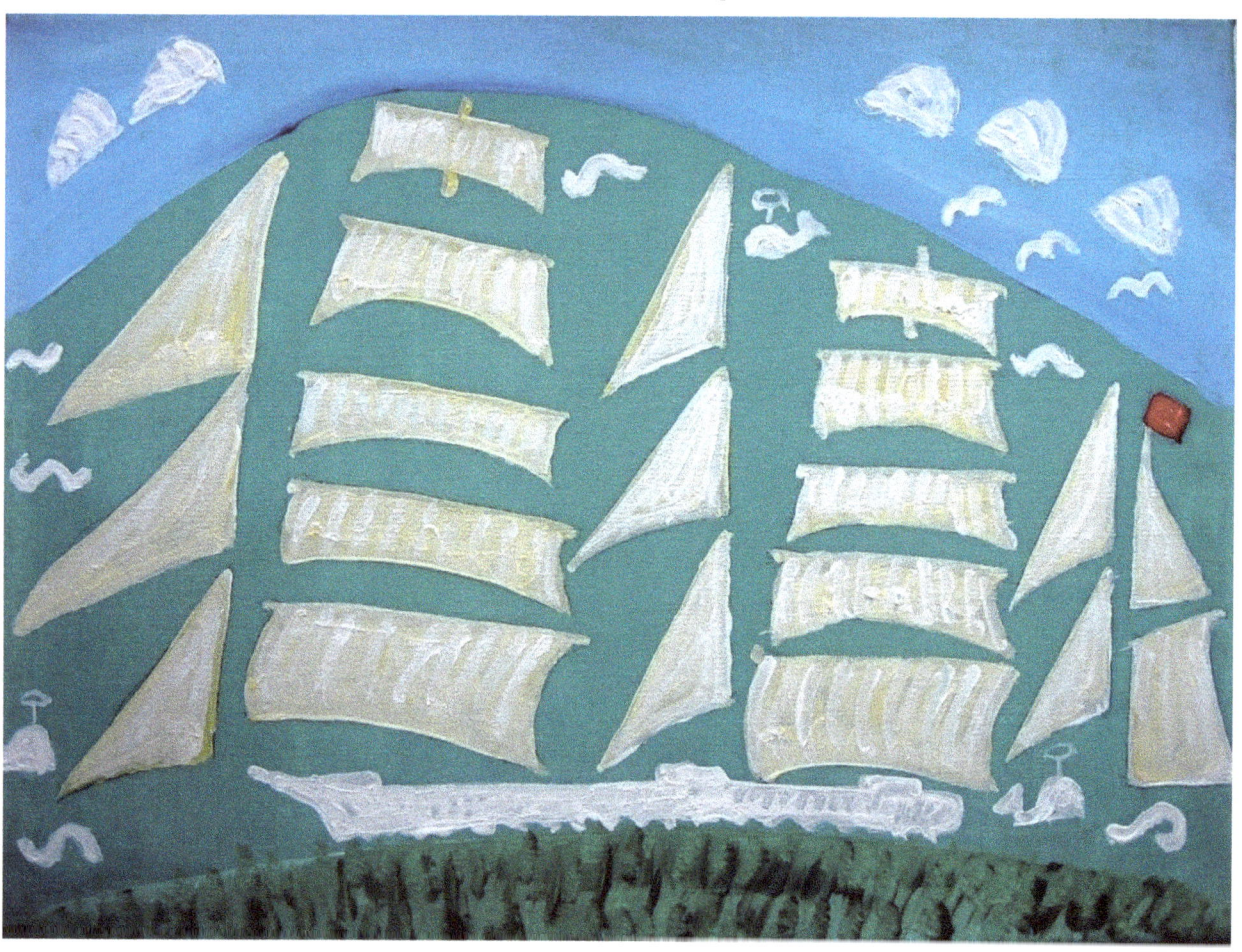

Ghost Ship (Breon O'Casey)

GHOST SHIP - painted in memory of local artist Breon O'Casey.

Gleaner

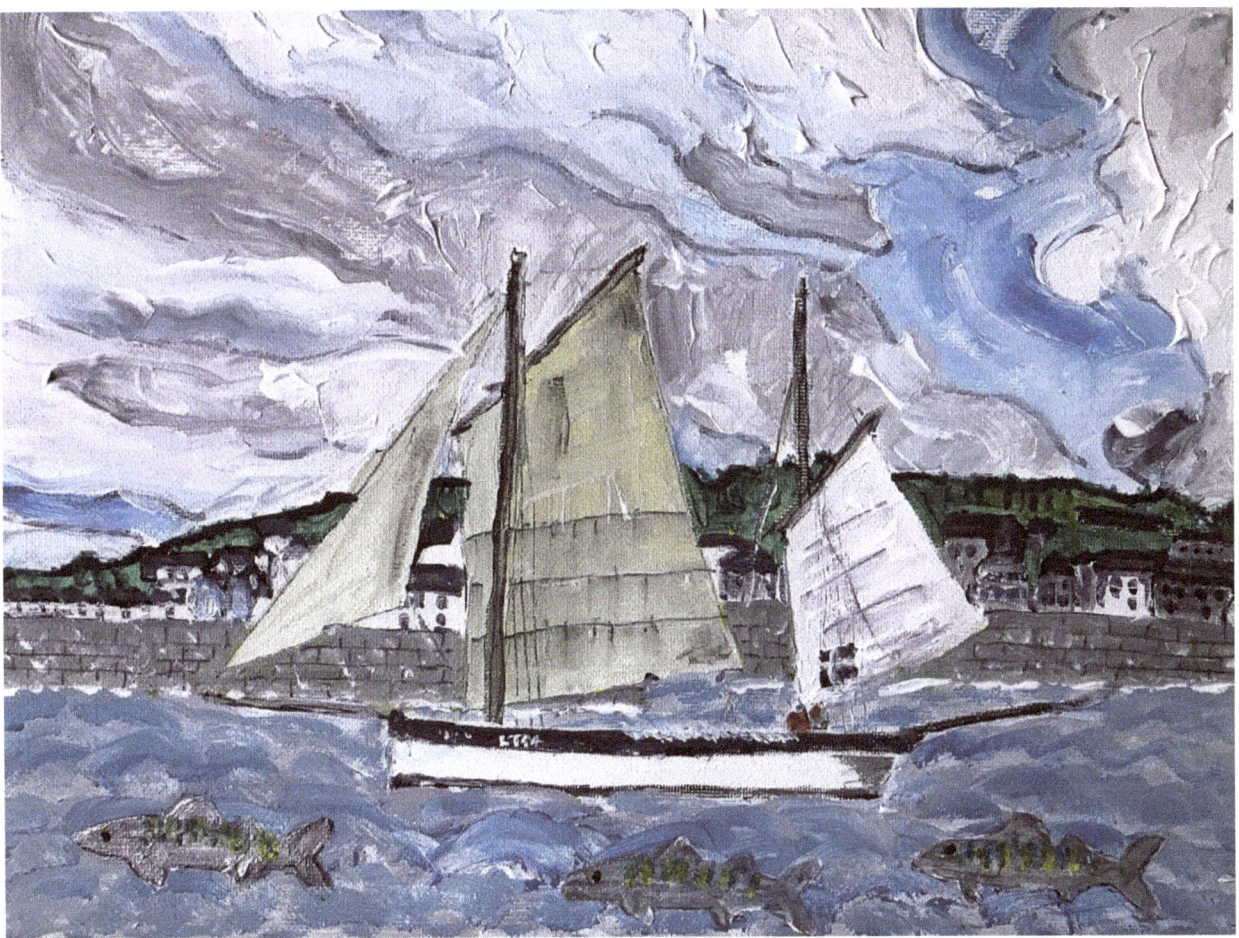

GLEANER - was built as a Lowestoft drifter of wooden carvel construction by Kitto of Porthleven in 1874 and at some point was taken to Germany where she was hauled ashore for restoration in the 1970s. This was not completed and the vessel was brought back to the UK by her present owner. Since then, Cornish shipwright Spike Davies saved her after the local council threatened to destroy her and he, with a team of helpers, dismantled the entire boat into a container, shipped her back to England and spent the next five years putting her back together. She sailed for the first time in 40 years in the summer of 2018.

The oldest industry at **Porthleven** is **fishing**, an occupation in which the same families have been engaged for many generations. The Cornish fishermen are considered to be among the most hardy and venturesome of the south coast fishermen.

Golden Hind

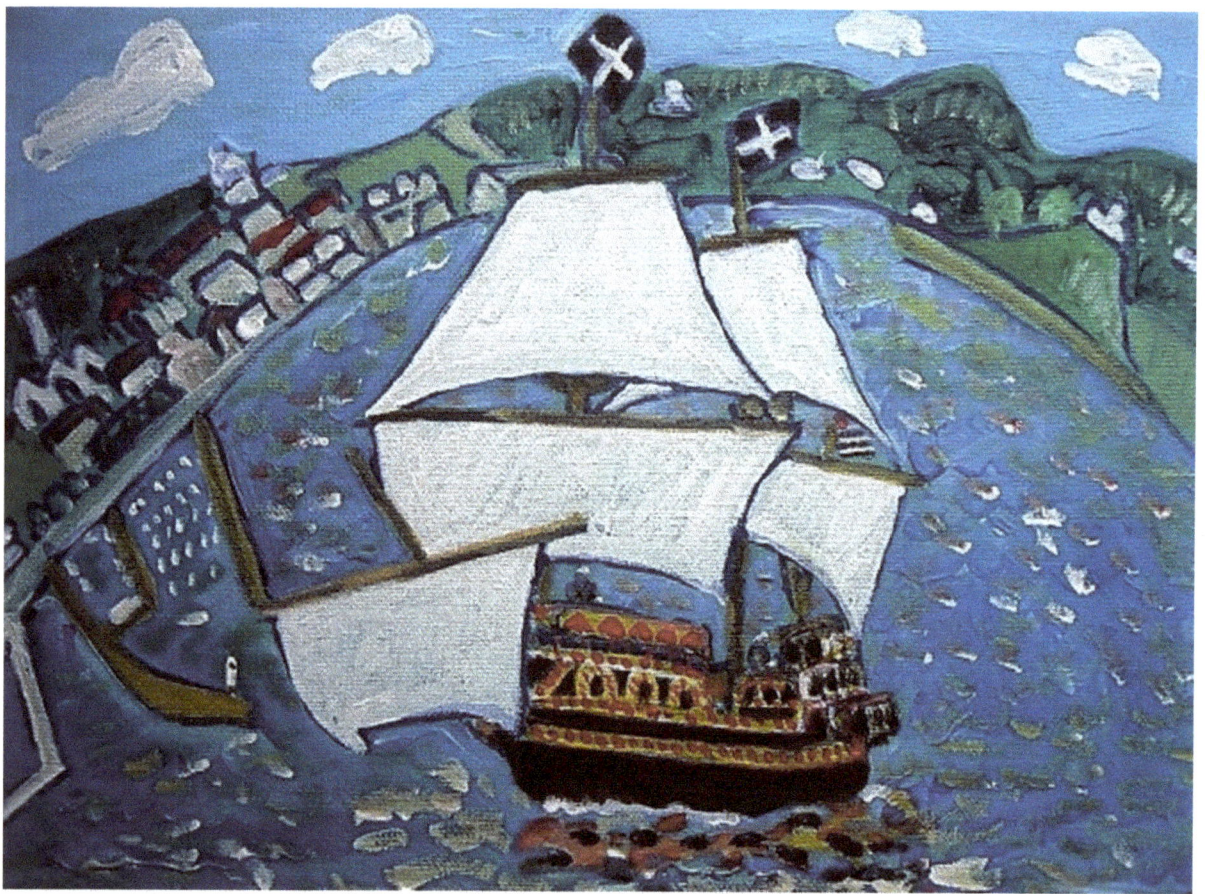

GOLDEN HIND - A replica of *Golden Hind* has been permanently moored in the harbour of the sea port of Brixham in Devon (50°23'48"N 3°30'46"W) since 1963 following its use in the TV series *Sir Francis Drake*, which was filmed in and around the bays of Torbay and Dartmouth. The replica ship used in the TV series cost the film studio £25,000 to construct and had no rear gallery or gun deck and was a converted fishing boat. The ship sank in heavy seas whilst under tow in 1987 to Dartmouth for restoration and could not be saved. A second, full-sized replica was completed in 1988 and stands in the harbour being visited by thousands of visitors annually.

Grace

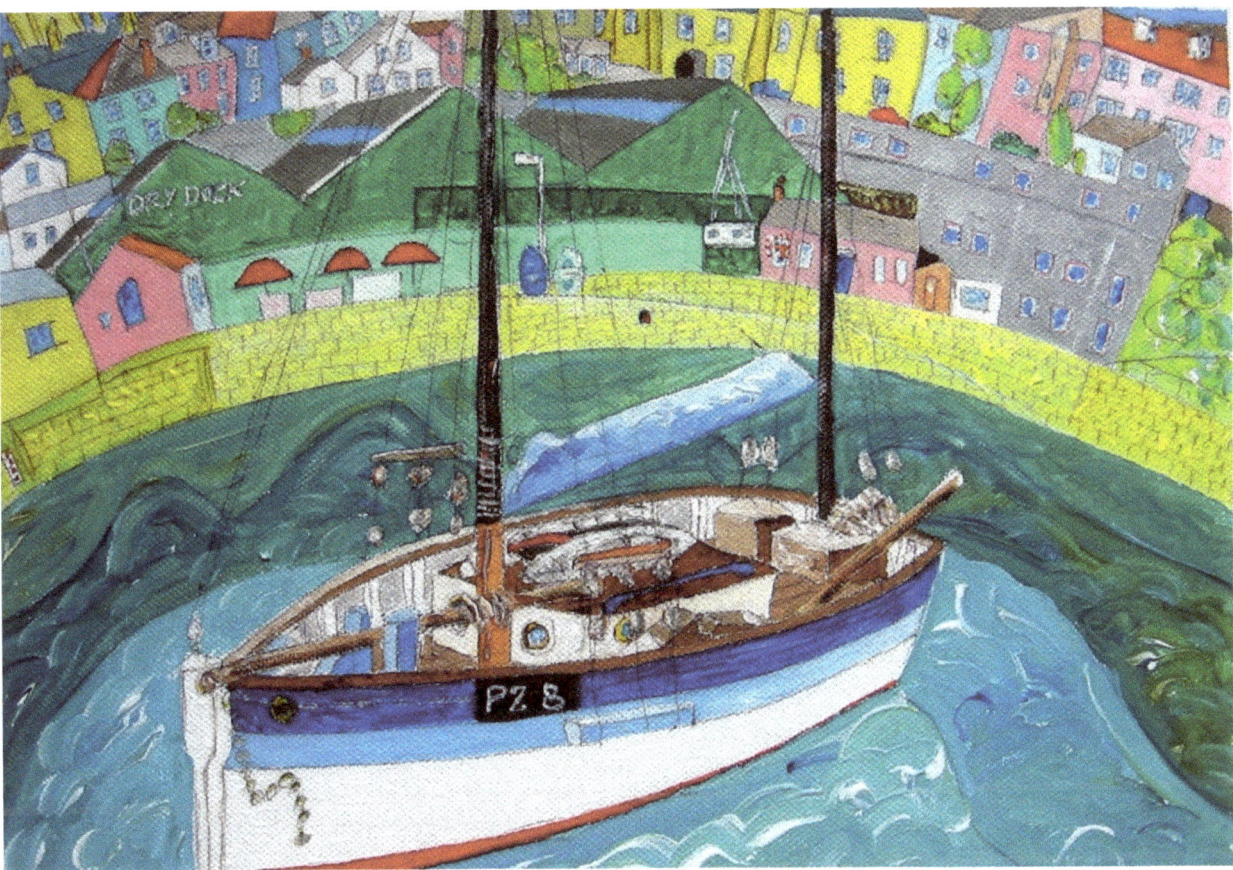

GRACE - Built in 1906 by Henry Roberts of Mevagissey **GRACE** is a **Cornish** fishing lugger with a carvel built hull of oak frames, a pitch pine deck and iroko planking. Her current engine is a Lister 3 Diesel made in 1945. ...She is now privately owned and is one of the few remaining **Cornish luggers** from the days of true working sail.

Grayhound

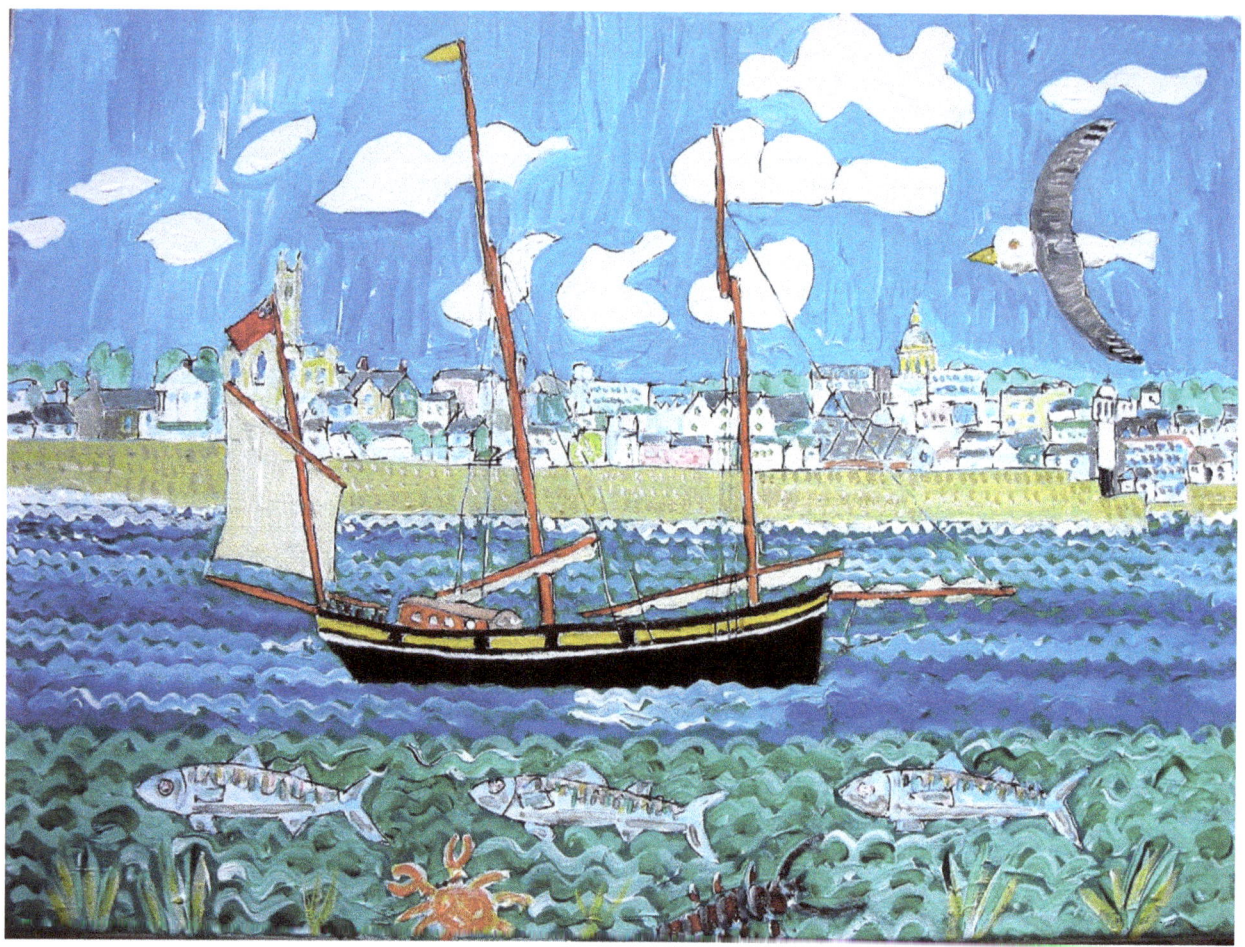

Grayhound approaches Penzance Harbour

GRAYHOUND - The story of S/V Grayhound – a replica 1776 Cornish Privateer Lugger. Grayhound was built using traditional methods in Millbrook, Cornwall in 2012. From her Atlantic adventures of 2014 to her sail cargo business of today, the crew of Grayhound have encouraged families and young professionals to sail with them providing a low carbon alternative to traditional cargo transport.

Grossheimherzogin Elisa

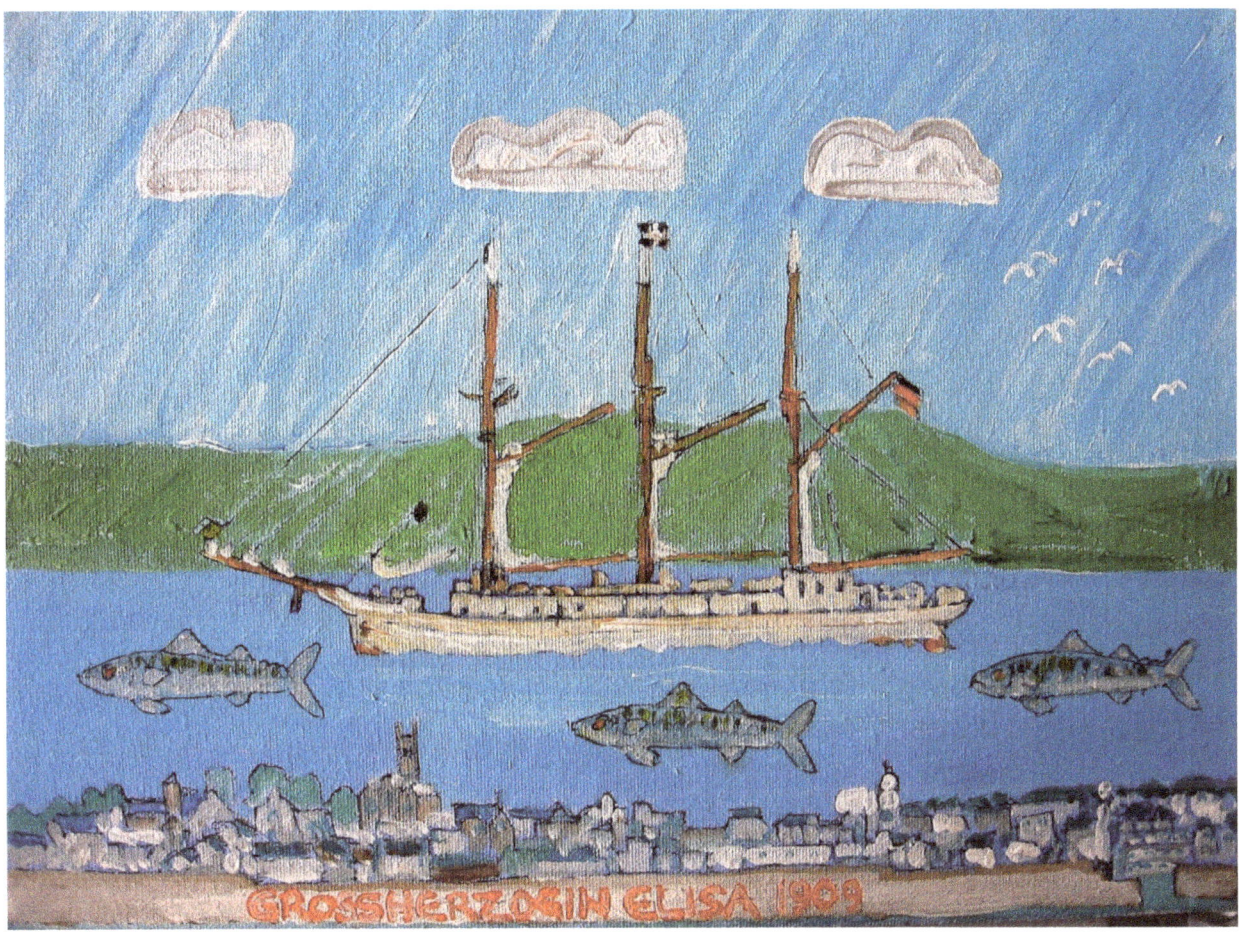

GROSSHERZOGIN ELISABETH - was built in 1909 as a trading schooner called San Antonio. In 1936, their rig was dismantled and her diesel engine was replaced with a stronger one. She then traded as a motor coaster until 1971 when she was sold to German owners who refitted the rig and reconstructed her to the sail passenger ship Ariadne. In 1982, An Elsfleth ship owner took her to her new home port, where she has been ever since, and used as a hostel and training ship for ship's mechanics and nautical officers.

Gry Maritha

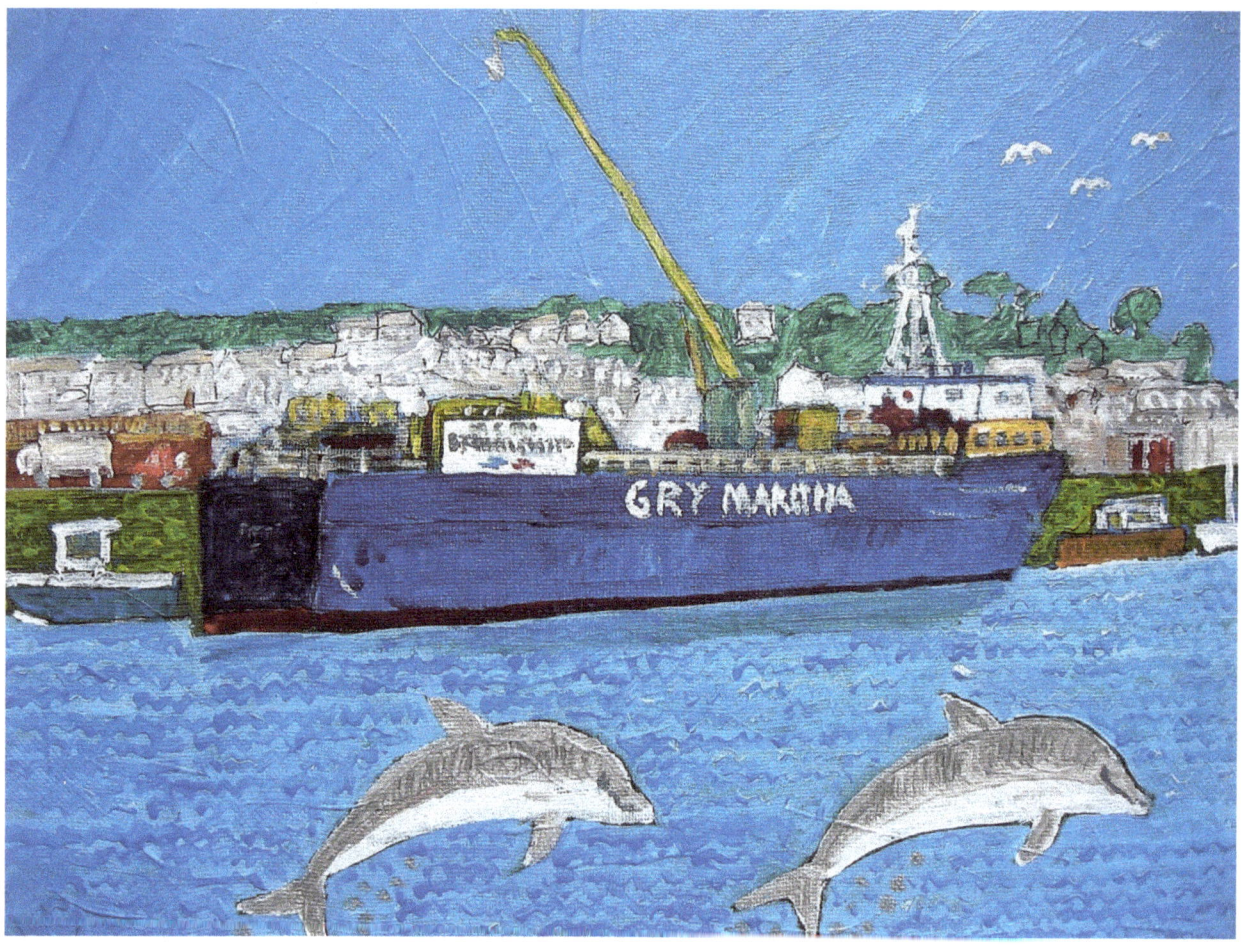

GRY MARITHA - is a freight ship based at Penzance in Cornwall, England, United Kingdom, run by the Isles of Scilly Steamship Company *Gry Maritha* was built by Moen Slip in Norway, in 1981. The ship was named after the daughter of the first captain, Tor Sevaldsen.

Guide Me

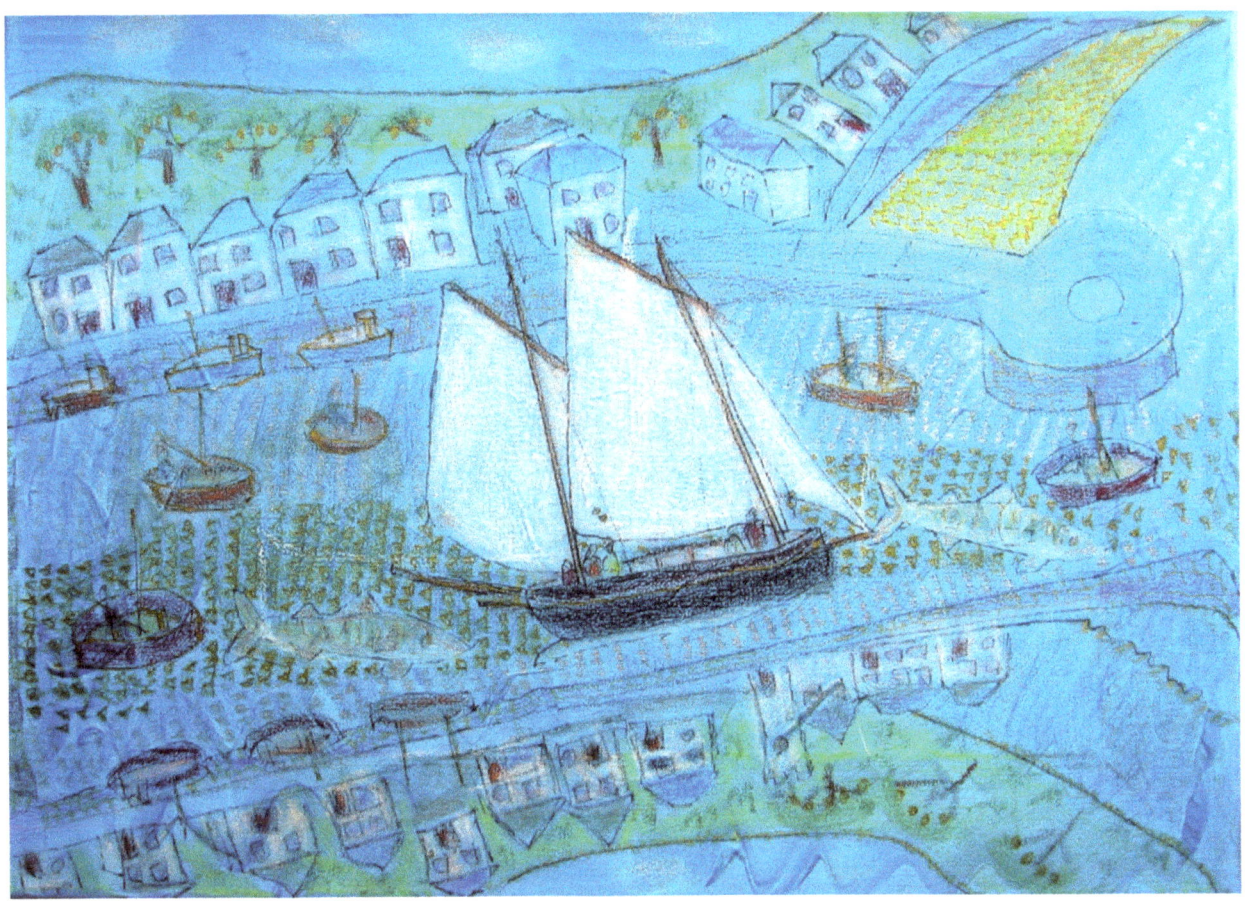

Looe lugger Guide Me, (Crayon on Canvass)

GUIDE ME - Built by Ferris at Looe in 1911 as a mackerel drifter. GUIDE ME worked out of Looe and Mevagissey until 1966. Purchased in 1977 by Judy Brickhill, and who sailed her in 1988 to South Africa via Brazil and returned to Cornwall in 1992. GUIDE ME is still in private ownership and is probably the most original Cornish Lugger. She has no engine.

Gulliver

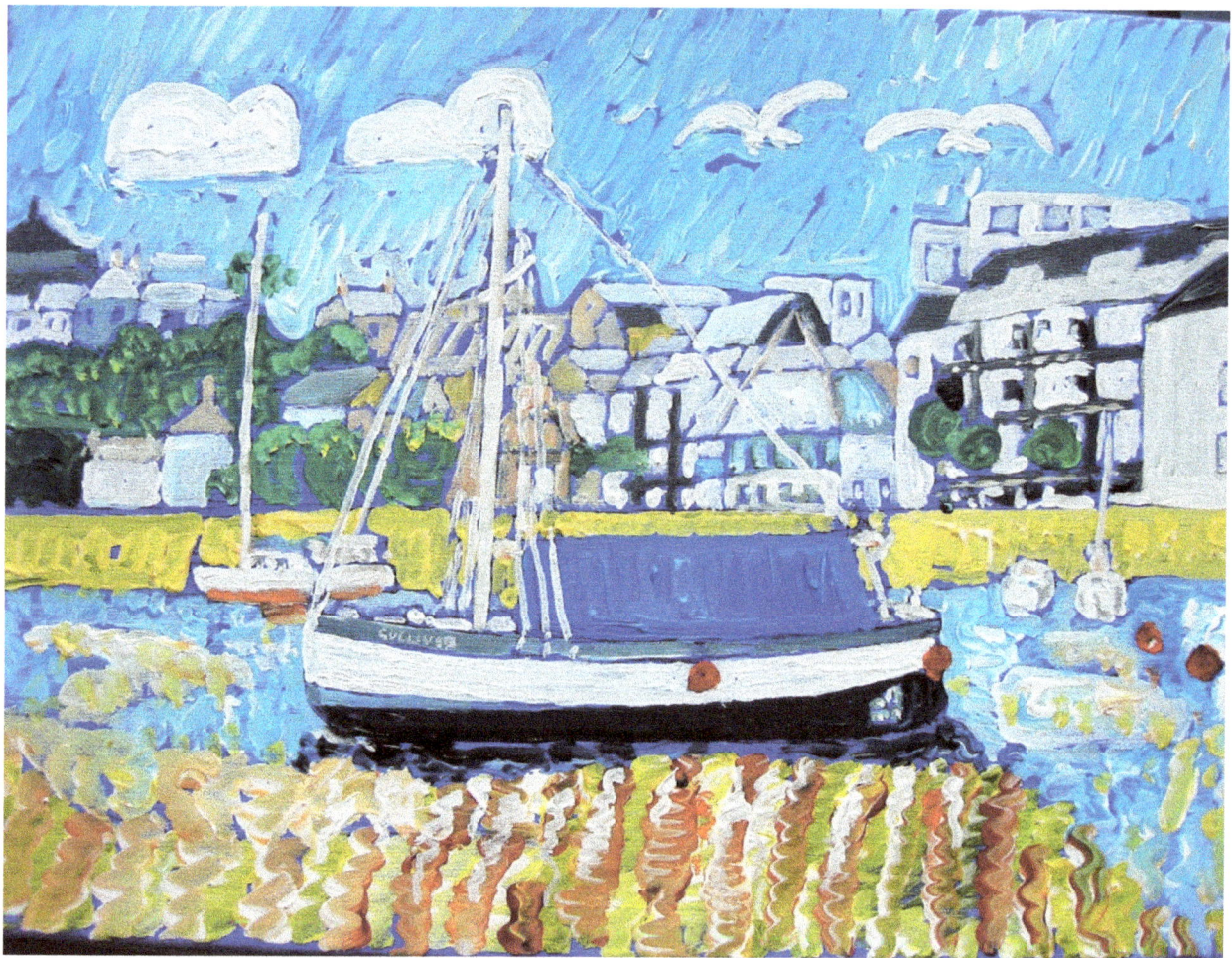

Gulliver on the drying mooring

Gulliver's Travels, or *Travels into Several Remote Nations of the World. In Four Parts. By Lemuel Gulliver, First a Surgeon, and then a Captain of Several Ships* is a 1726 prose satire by the Anglo-Irish writer and clergyman Jonathan Swift, satirising both human nature and the "travellers' tales" literary subgenre. It is Swift's best-known full-length work and a classic of English literature. Swift claimed that he wrote *Gulliver's Travels* "to vex the world rather than divert it".

Happy Return

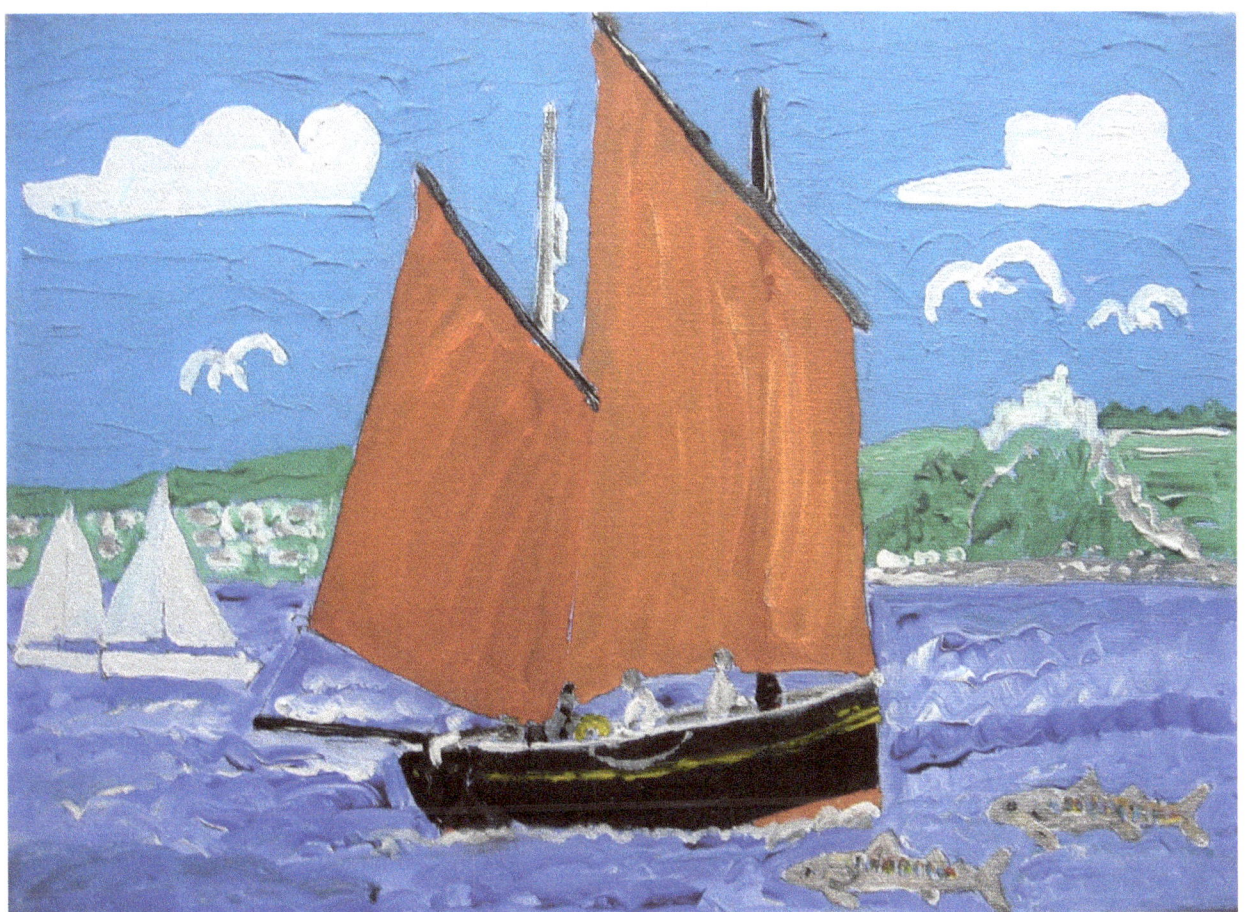

Happy Return off the North Arm

HAPPY RETURN is a **Cornish Lugger** built in Porthleven in 1905 and now based in Penzance. It was restored by the Mounts Bay **Lugger** Association (MBLA) in 1995 and is now in full working order with an active sailing program each year that takes it to Brittany, Ireland, and Scilly Isles along the South Coast of England.

Happy Return

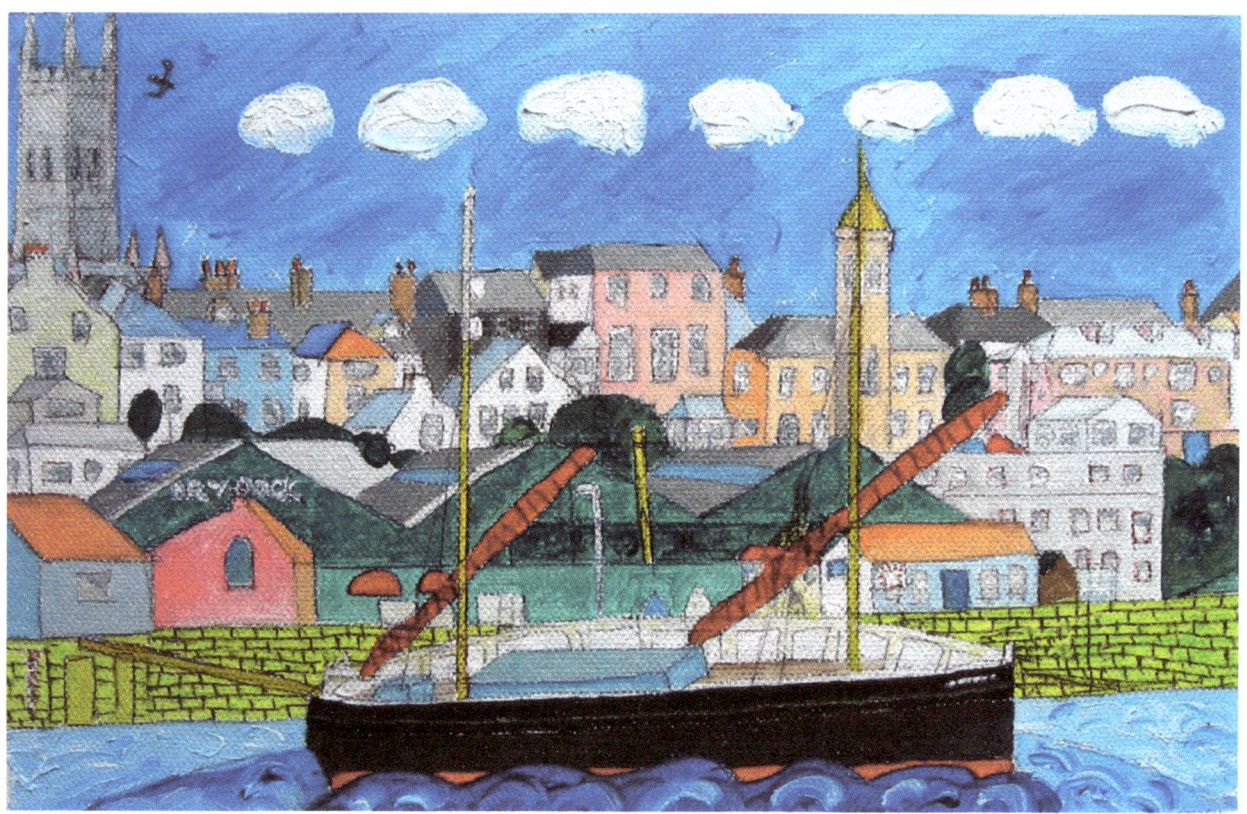

Happy Return off the North Arm

Hear the Sea

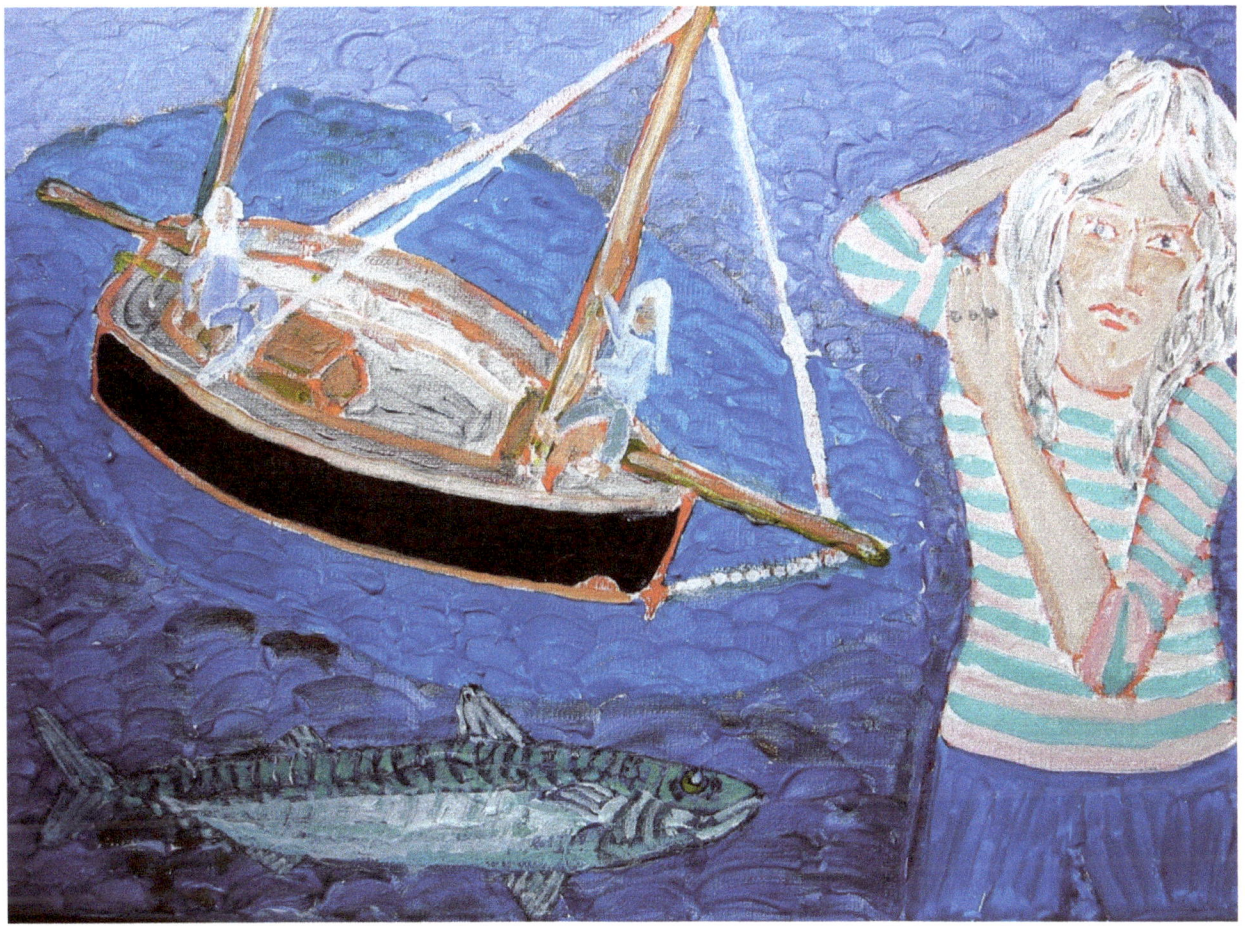

Can you hear the waves? Hear the sea.

Storms cause £4m damage in Cornwall 4 February **2014** Sea defences, walls and footpaths have been damaged, including at Newlyn Green.

Herring gull story

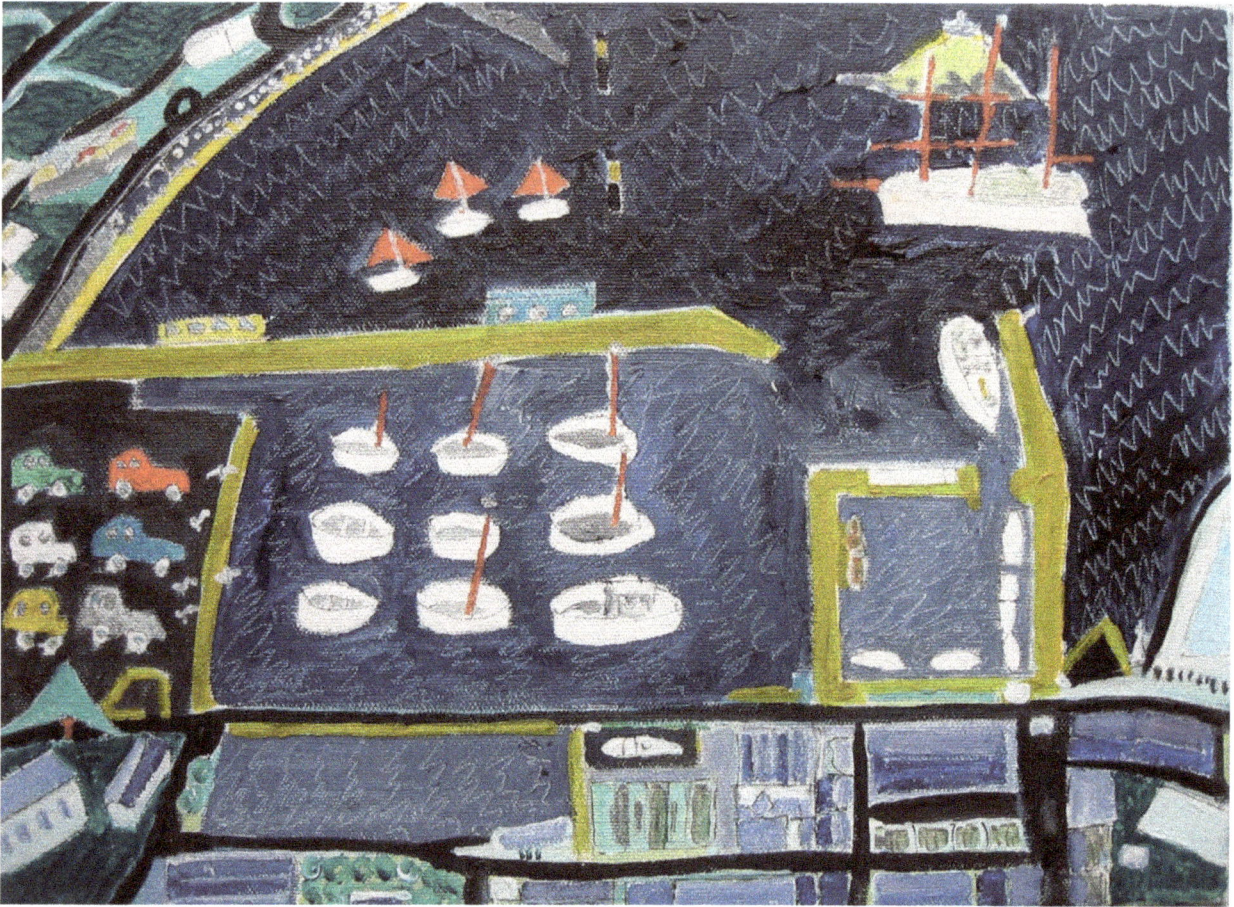

Herring gull scientific name: Larus argentatus the **herring gull** is the typical 'seagull' of our seaside resorts, though our coastal populations have declined in recent decades. Species information Category Seabirds Statistics Length: 55-67cm Wingspan: 130-150cm Weight: 690-1440g Average lifespan: 12 years.

Irene

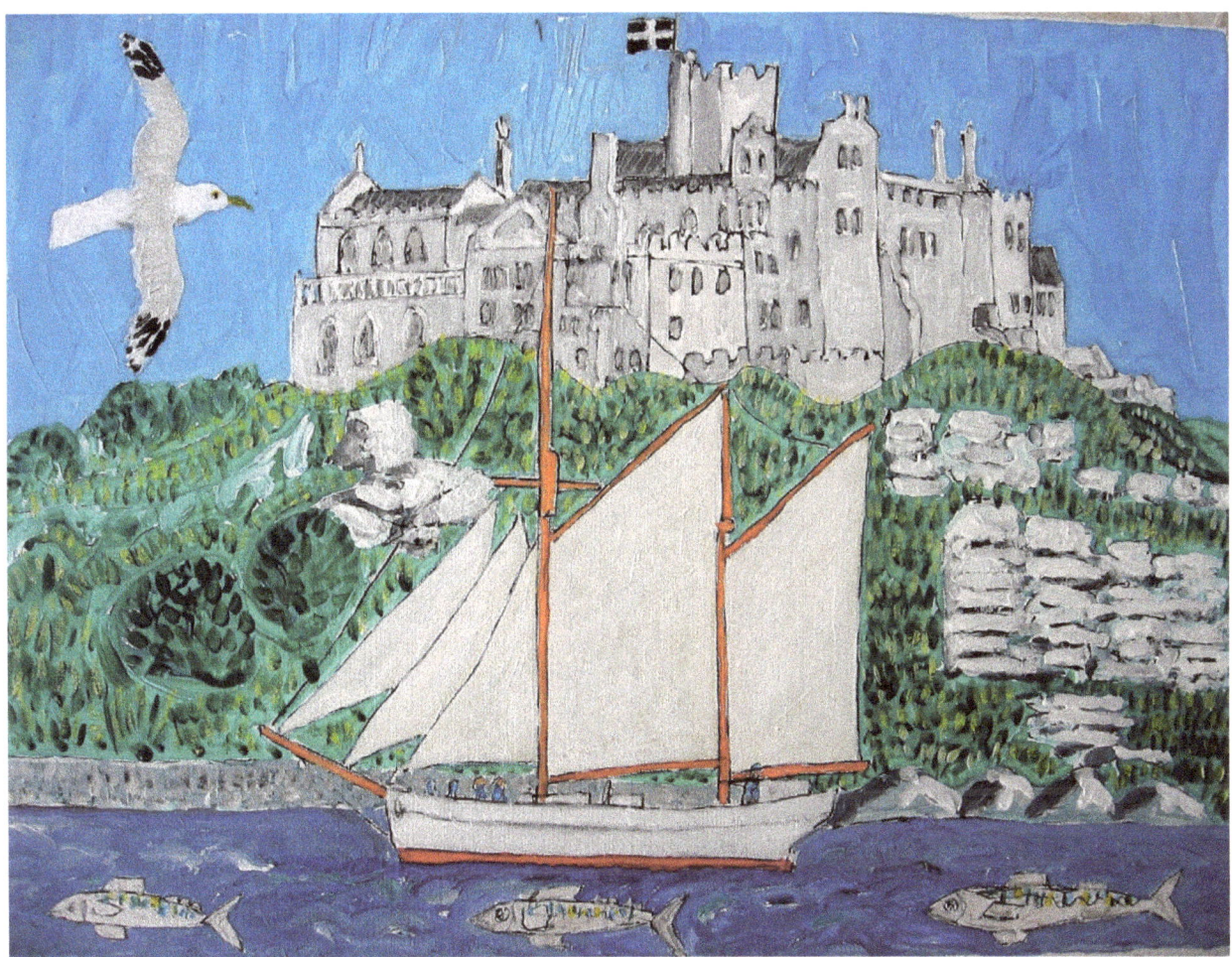

IRENE - On 29 May 1907 Irene was launched at the Bridgwater yard of F J Carver & Sons, who had started building her on their own account. Whilst on the stocks she was sold to Colthurst Symons, a local brick and tile manufacturer, and was named after his daughter, Irene. Her hull was framed in oak and planked with pitch pine; the keel and garboard strake were of elm and the keelson of greenheart. Galvanised black iron was used to fasten her throughout. The top strakes and the covering board (the wide timber at the edge of the deck) were of greenheart and chestnut, to help withstand rough handling at the quayside. Irene loaded her first cargo on 17 June 1907, less than three weeks after her launch, and carried it from Bridgwater to Penzance.

Johanna Lucretia

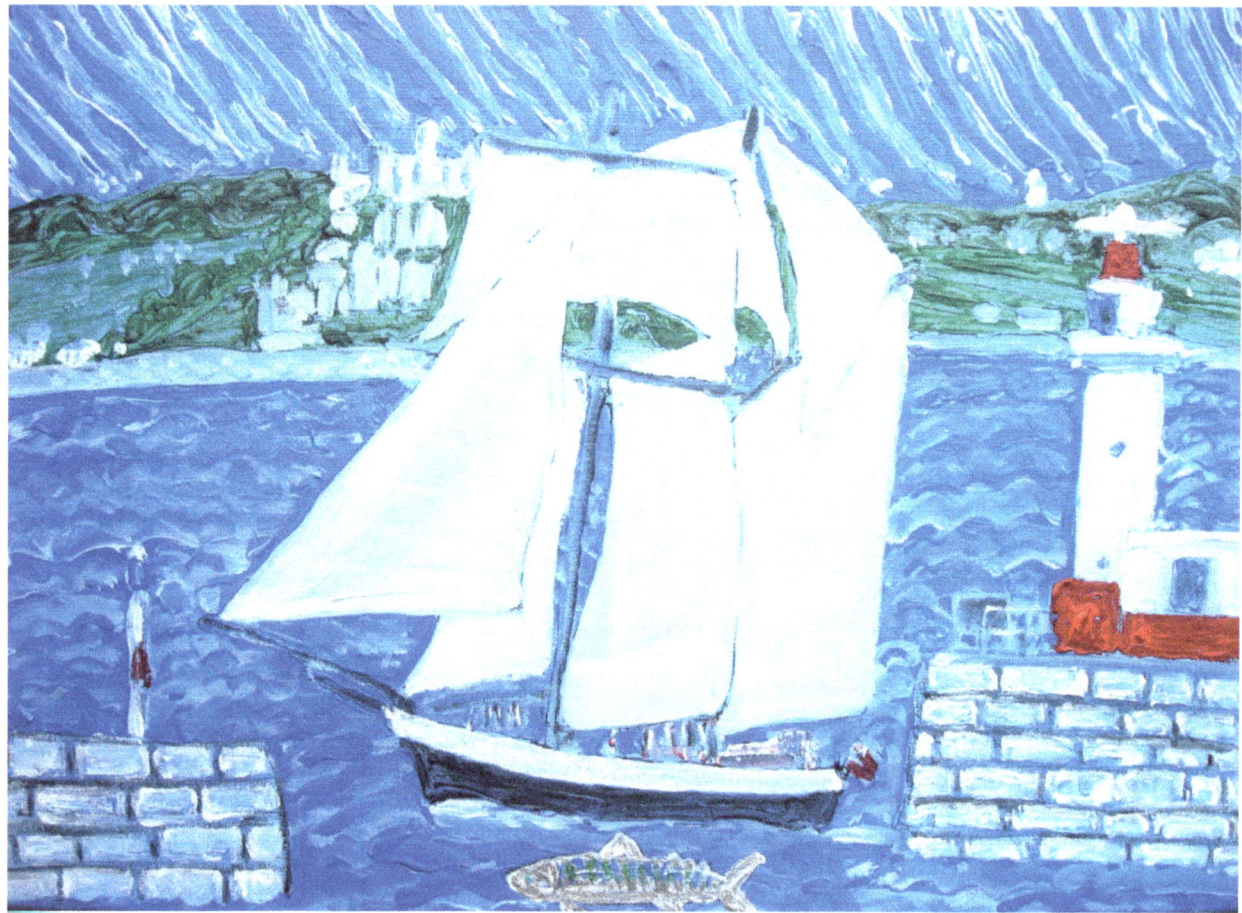

JOHANNA LUCRETIA - Johanna Lucretia is solidly built, with oak hull planking laid on extremely strong oak frames and an iroko deck. Three separate watertight bulkheads mean there is the potential for longer distance cruising in the future. As a schooner, she has two masts, which are pine, stayed traditionally with lanyards and deadeyes. On the foremast she can set two square sails in addition to her gaff rigged fore and aft sails.

John's Boys

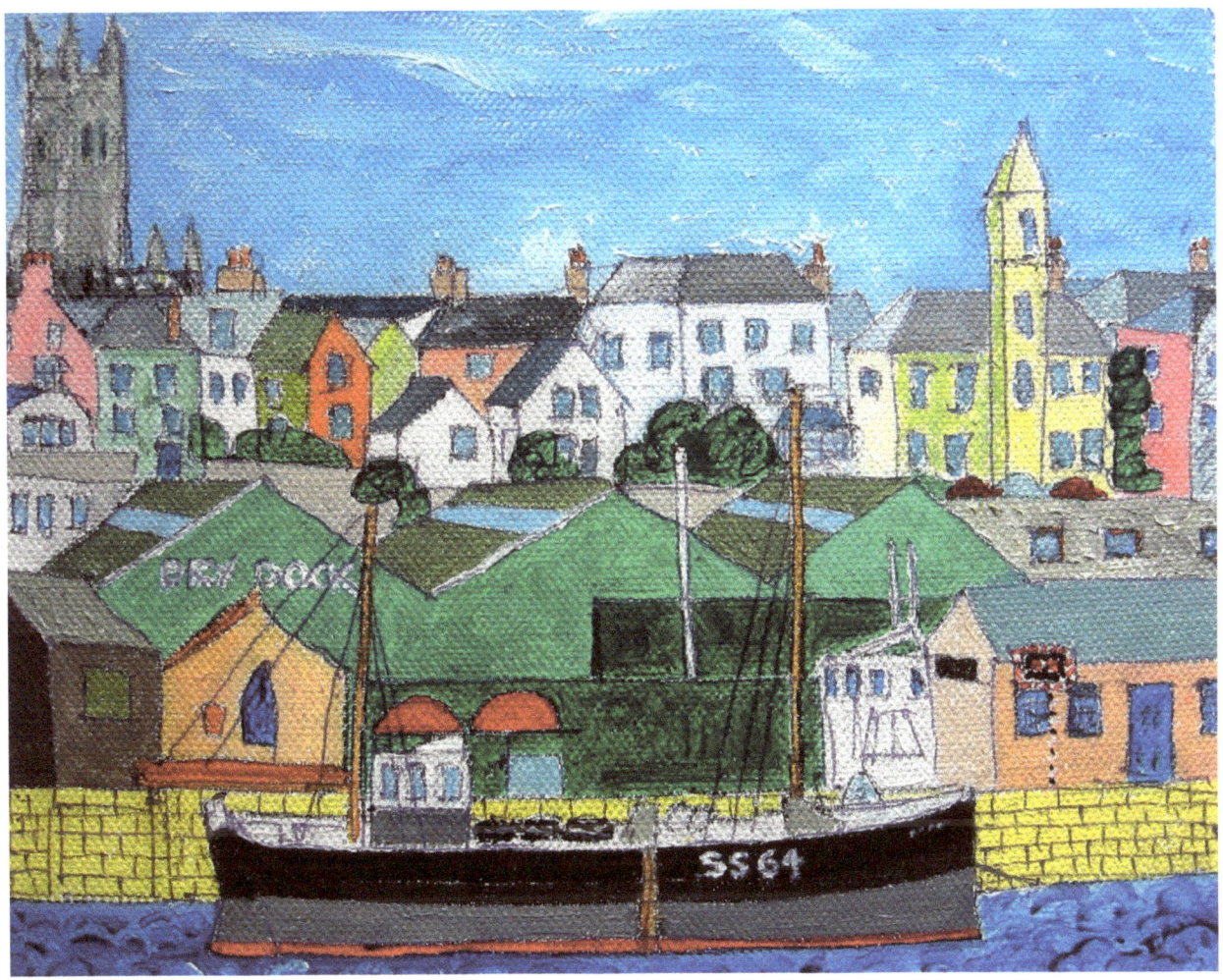

In Penzance

Juno

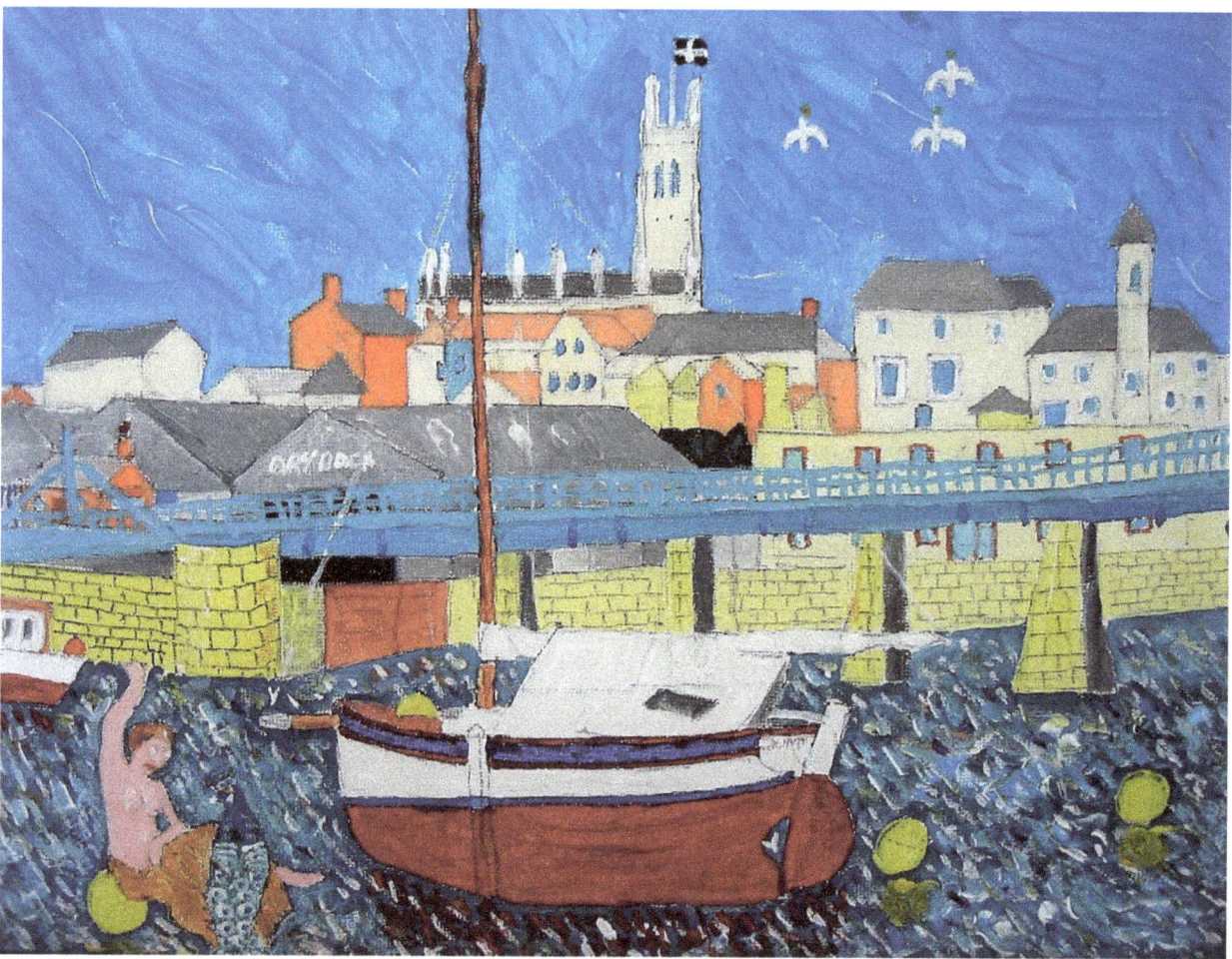

Juno on the drying mooring

JUNO - Built in Porthleven, Cornwall in 1971 by a local shipwright as his own boat. Found on the beach in St Just in the 1980's she underwent a decade long rebuild, finally being launched in March 1993. She then won first prize in the Amateur Boatbuilding competition at the Wooden Boat Show in London of that year, a testament to the quality of the rebuild work carried out by her owner over the previous 10 years.

Kara Mor and Karina Olsen

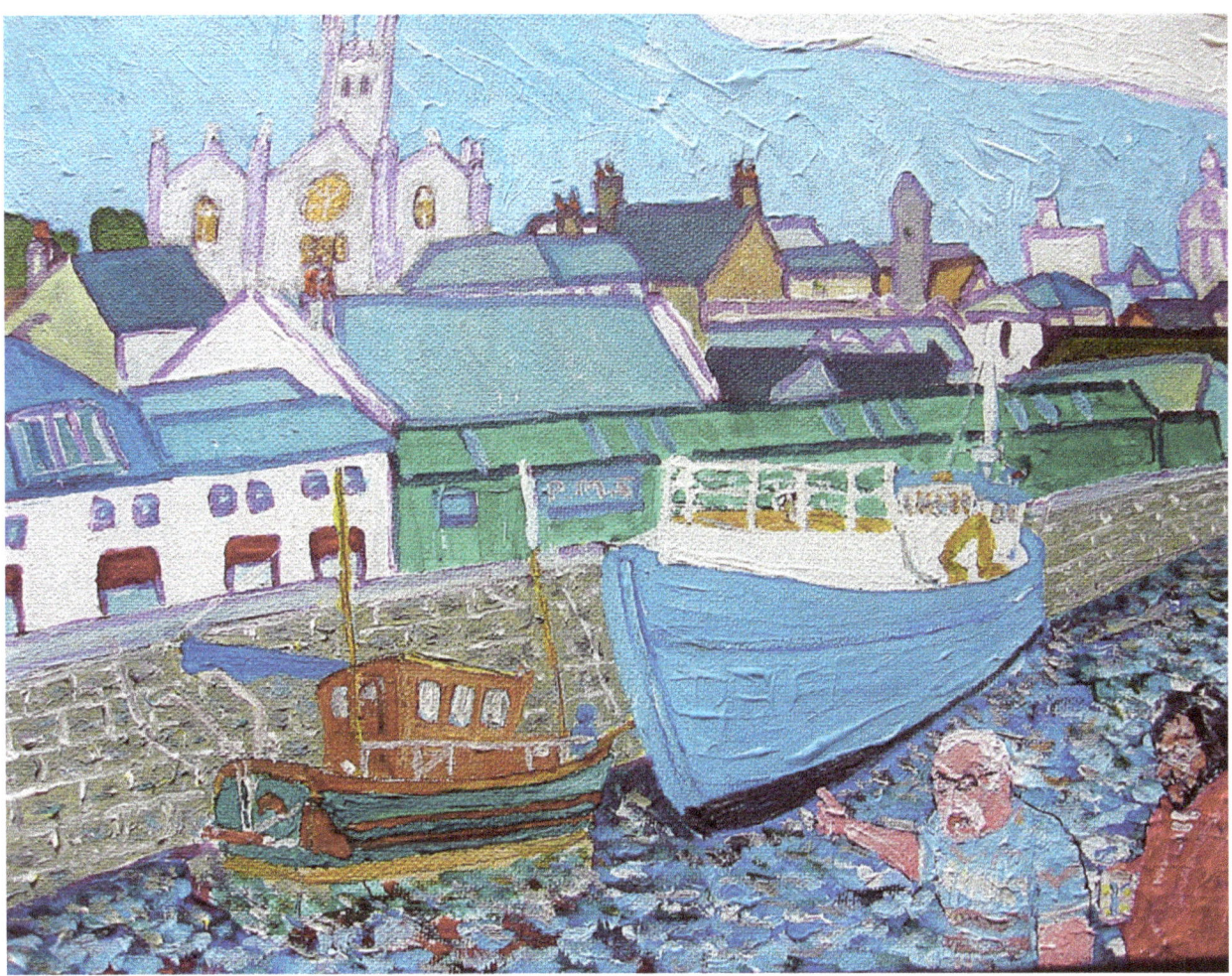

[Kara Mor and] **KARINA OLSEN** - These anchor seiners used to make trips up to three weeks using a seine net fishing mainly for plaice in the North Sea. They were capable of riding out appalling weather when lying at anchor - the bunks in for'ard accommodation had sliding doors to keep their occupants from falling out!

Kinsmen of the Wind

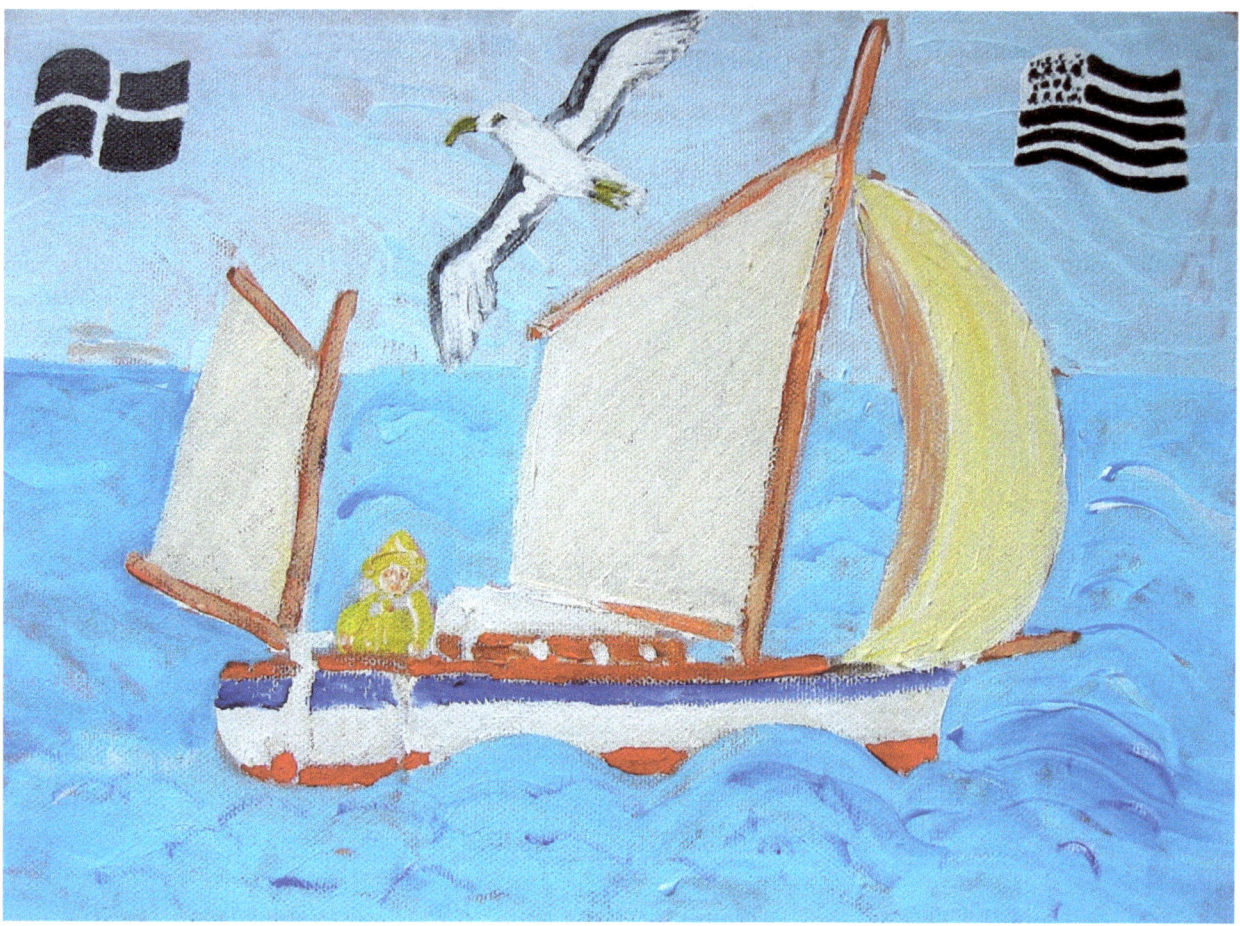

KINSMEN OF THE WIND - The duties of the Wind are few, to cast the ships, at Sea, Establish March, the Floods escort, and usher Liberty. By Emily Dickenson.

Klevia

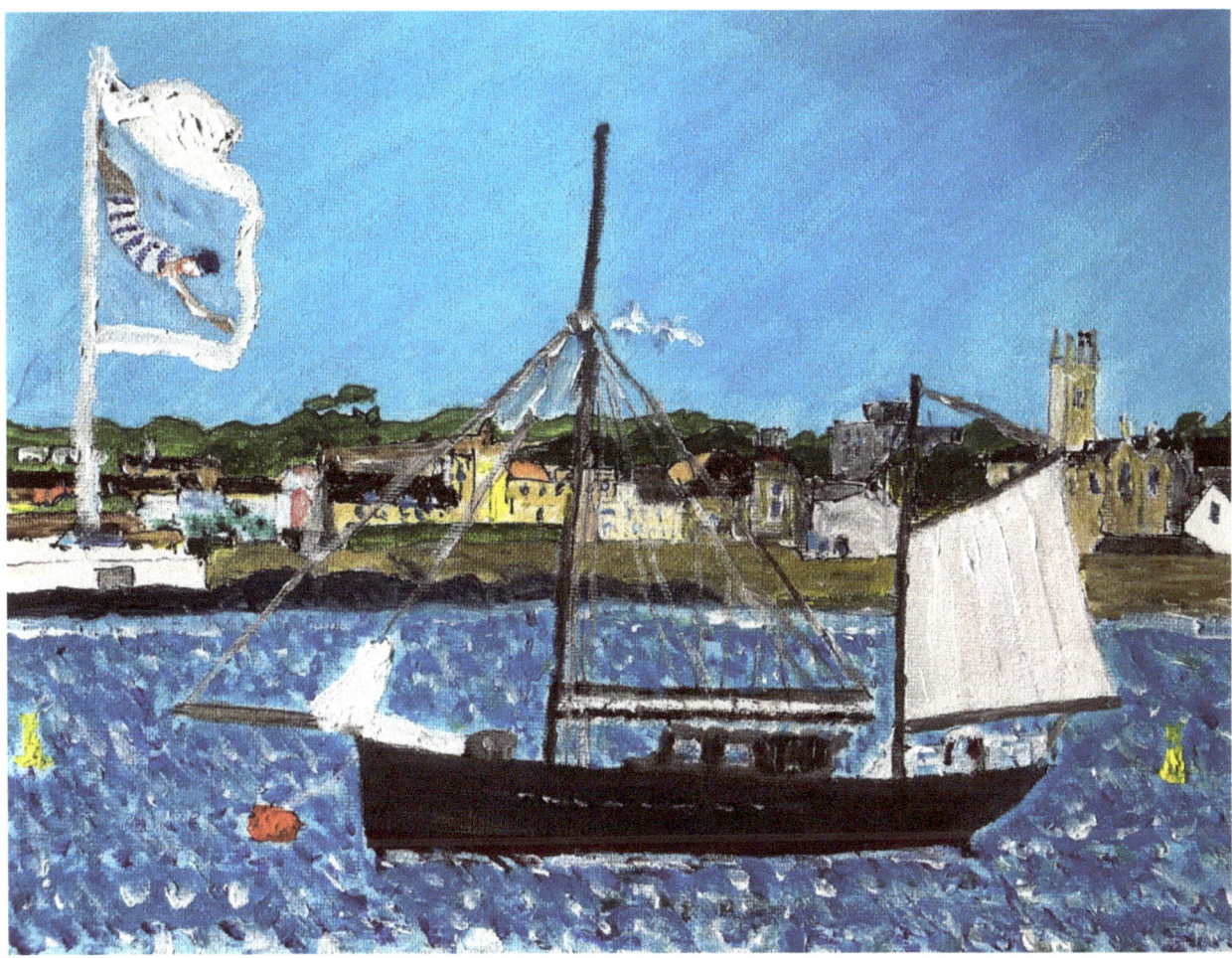

Klevia Built in Esbjerg, Denmark in 1936 for fishing the North Sea. Restored and traditionally rigged as a gaff ketch.

Lady of Avenel

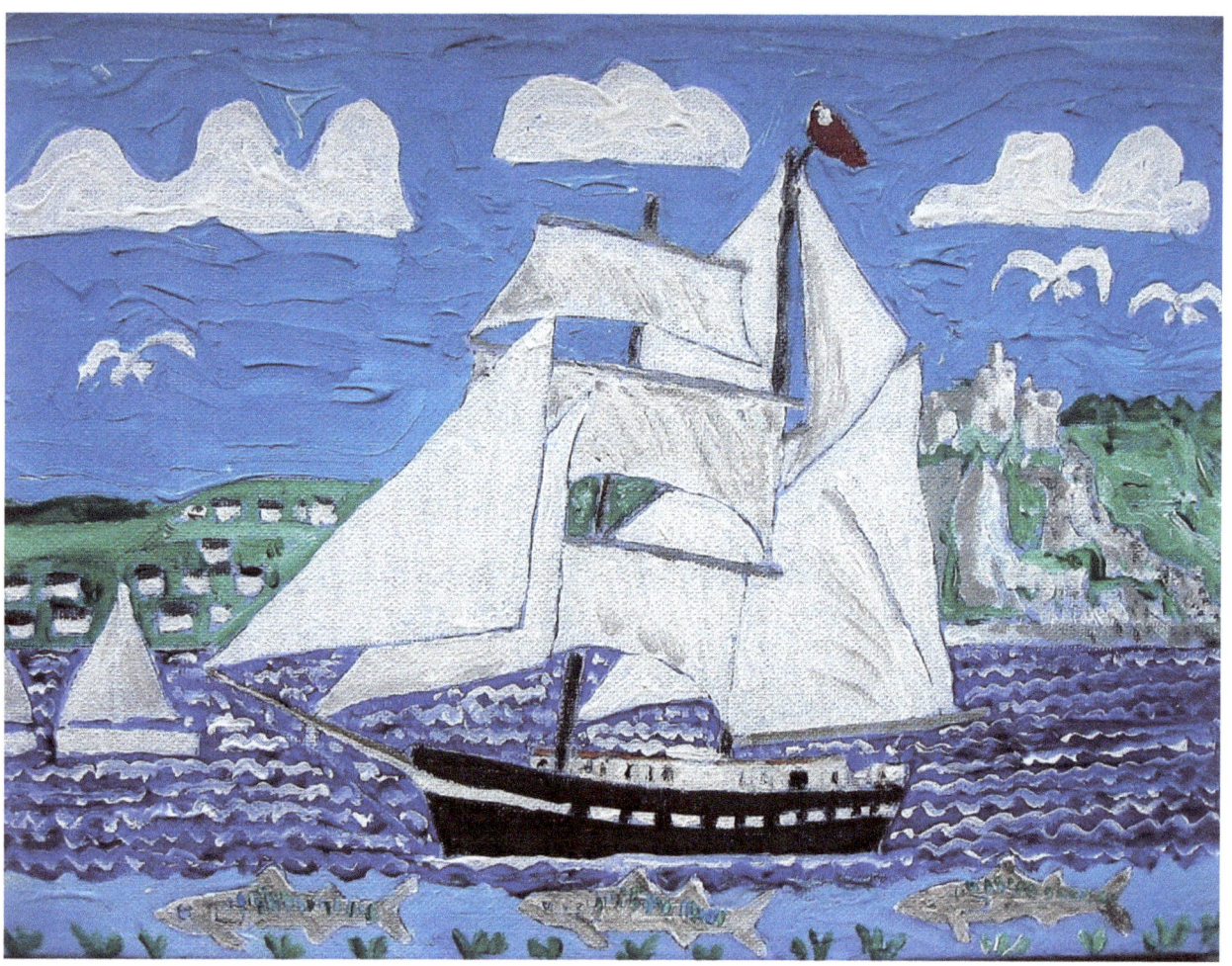

Lady of Avenel off the Mount

THE LADY OF AVENEL is a 102ft Brigantine square rigged ship with 12 guest berths.

Le Belem

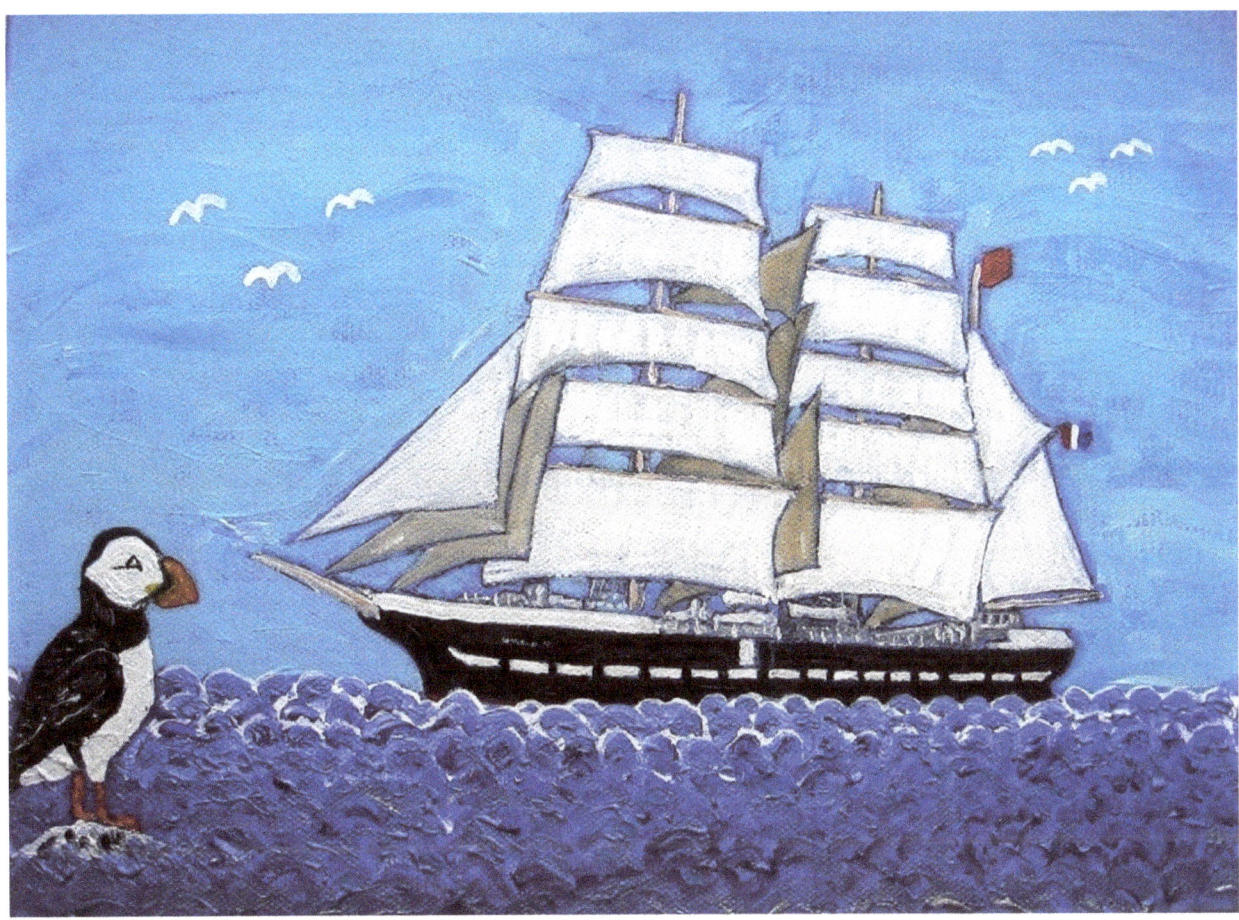

LE BELEM - Having begun life as a cargo ship transporting sugar from the West Indies as well as cocoa and coffee from Brazil and French Guiana to Nantes in France, the tall ship Belem is now over 120 years old, with a history that also includes becoming a private yacht for Hugh Grosvenor, 2nd Duke of Westminster (who renamed her Fantome II) and even sailing the seven seas under ownership of beer baron Sir Arthur Ernest Guinness.

Little Gem and Minerva

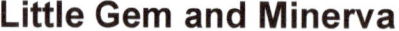

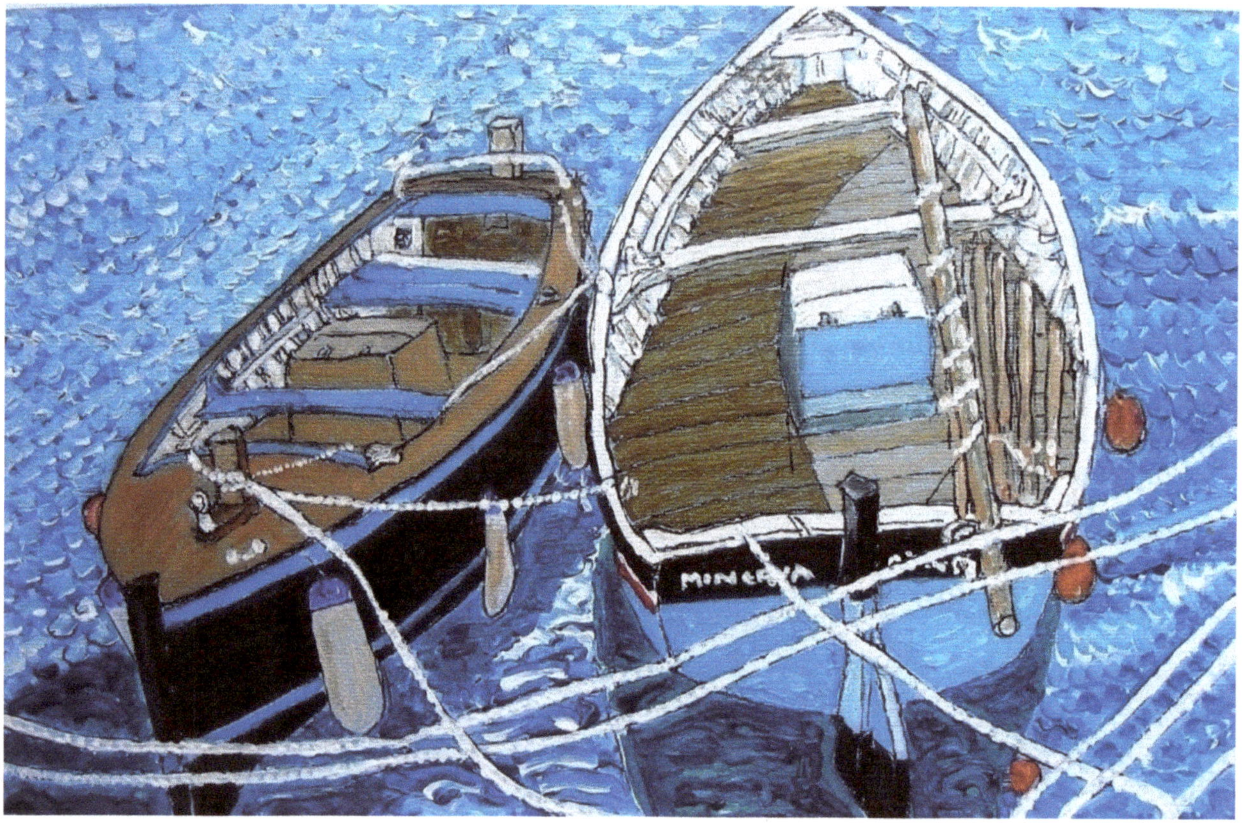

Little Gem – This Mevagissey tosher was built in 1906 by Fraziers yard, who produced a staggering amount of coastal inshore fishing boats during the early part of the last century. She is 18 feet long, with a beam of 6ft, and typical of the hundreds of boats that fished the east Cornwall coast in the last century. Originally built for the Lakeman family of Mevagissey, she was used for plummeting for mackerel, and would probably have gone netting also. Although the lines are typical of boats along the south-east Cornwall coast, toshers were mostly built at under 20 feet in length to avoid the higher bracket of harbour dues in Mevagissey.

Minerva see the history on film at you tube

Pilot Gig Longships

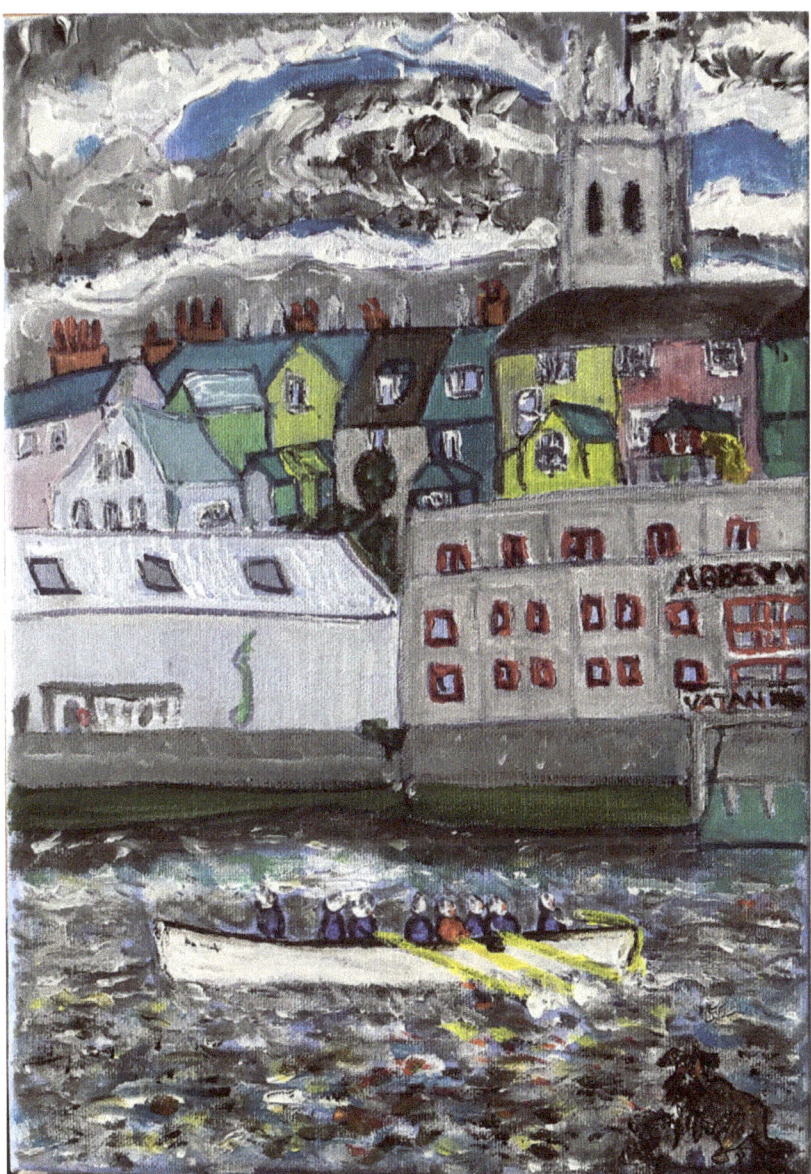

Cape Cornwall pilot Club

Abbey Basin. Quays and slipway. Circa early-mid 19th century. Dressed granite quays on the north, west and south side of Abbey Basin, with slipway and granite bollards on west side. The later causeway and the 1881 Ross Swing Bridge, rebuilt in 1981, on the east side of Abbey Basin are not included. The 1900 dry dock on the south side and Abbey Warehouse on the west side are separately included. Part of an unusually complete group of harbour structures in Penzance.

Cape Cornwall Pilot Gig Club! Established in 1989, we are a small and friendly gig club based at Sennen Cove at the far west of Cornwall. We also row regularly from Penzance Harbour.

Luggers racing off the prom

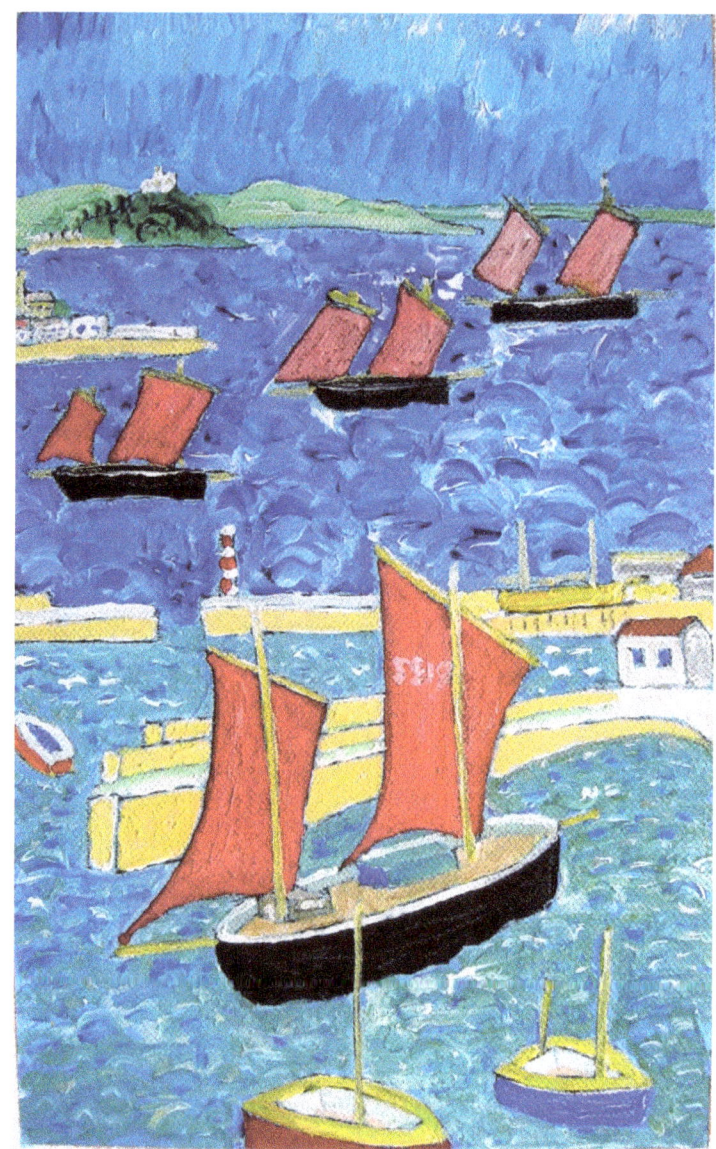

THE LUGGER - was the workhorse of the Cornish fishing fleet for over 200 years. Two distinct variants emerged; their design based upon whether they were to be used for fishing in the harsh waters of the Atlantic or the calmer waters of the Channel. In the west, the Mount's Bay lugger was built double-ended to deal with the rough Atlantic conditions and to enable it's fishermen to be able to hold a much larger catch.

Mount's Bay is the biggest bay in Cornwall. Its half-moon shape is similar to that of Donegal Bay in Ireland and Cardigan Bay in Wales, although, unlike the aforementioned bays, Mount's Bay is relatively sheltered from the prevailing Atlantic westerly's. However, it is a danger to shipping during onshore southerly and south-easterly gales.

Luke's Minnie

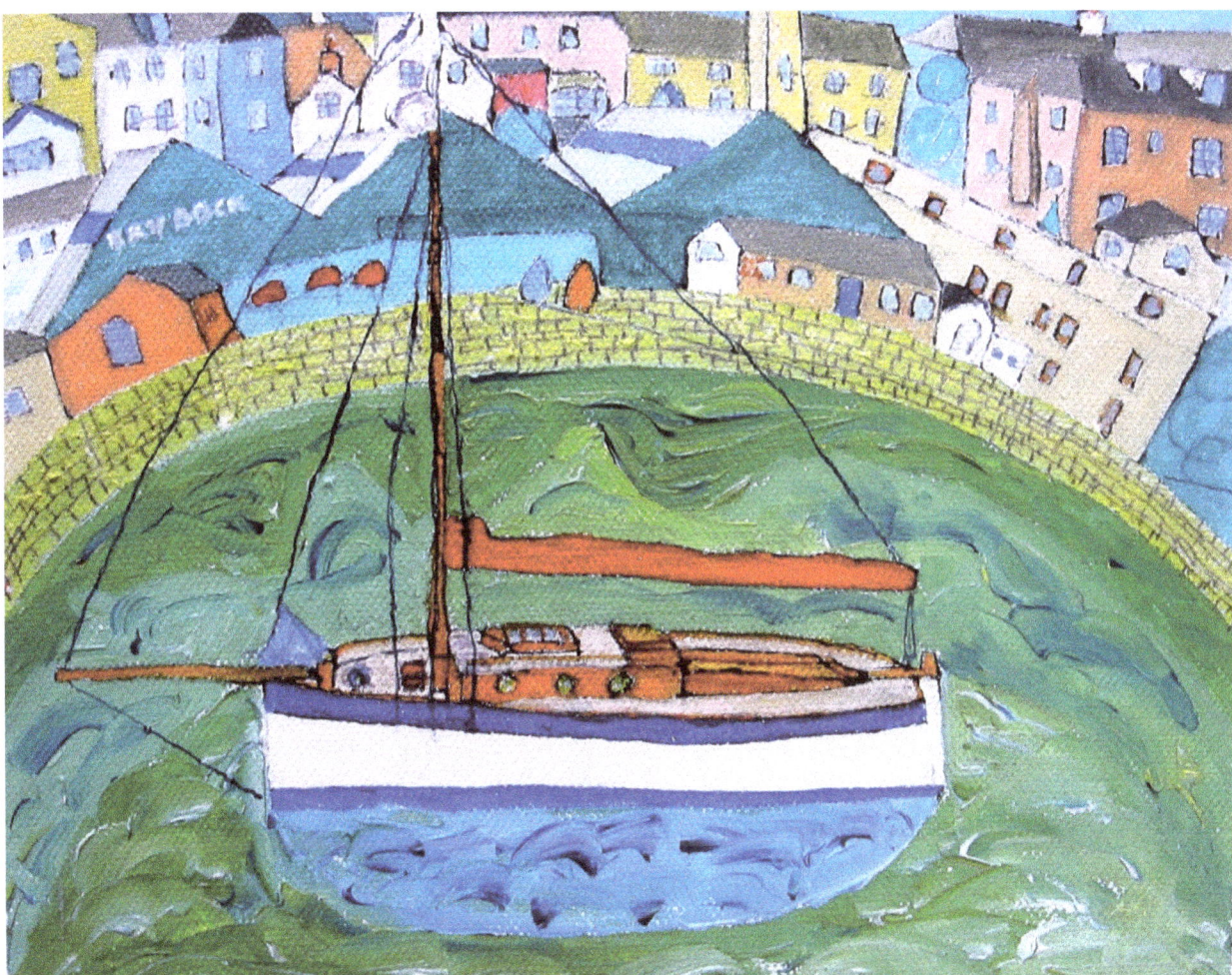

'MINNIE' - was built on Channel Pilot Cutter lines by Luke of the Hamble in 1893 as a gentleman's yacht. She was commissioned by Charles Harry Card of Vodoss House, Banister Road, Southampton who registered her at Lloyds on 28th March 1893 and claimed his occupation to be 'gentleman'. It is known that she has remained in commission as a private yacht ever since, more or less, and each owner has continued her registration.

Mali Rose

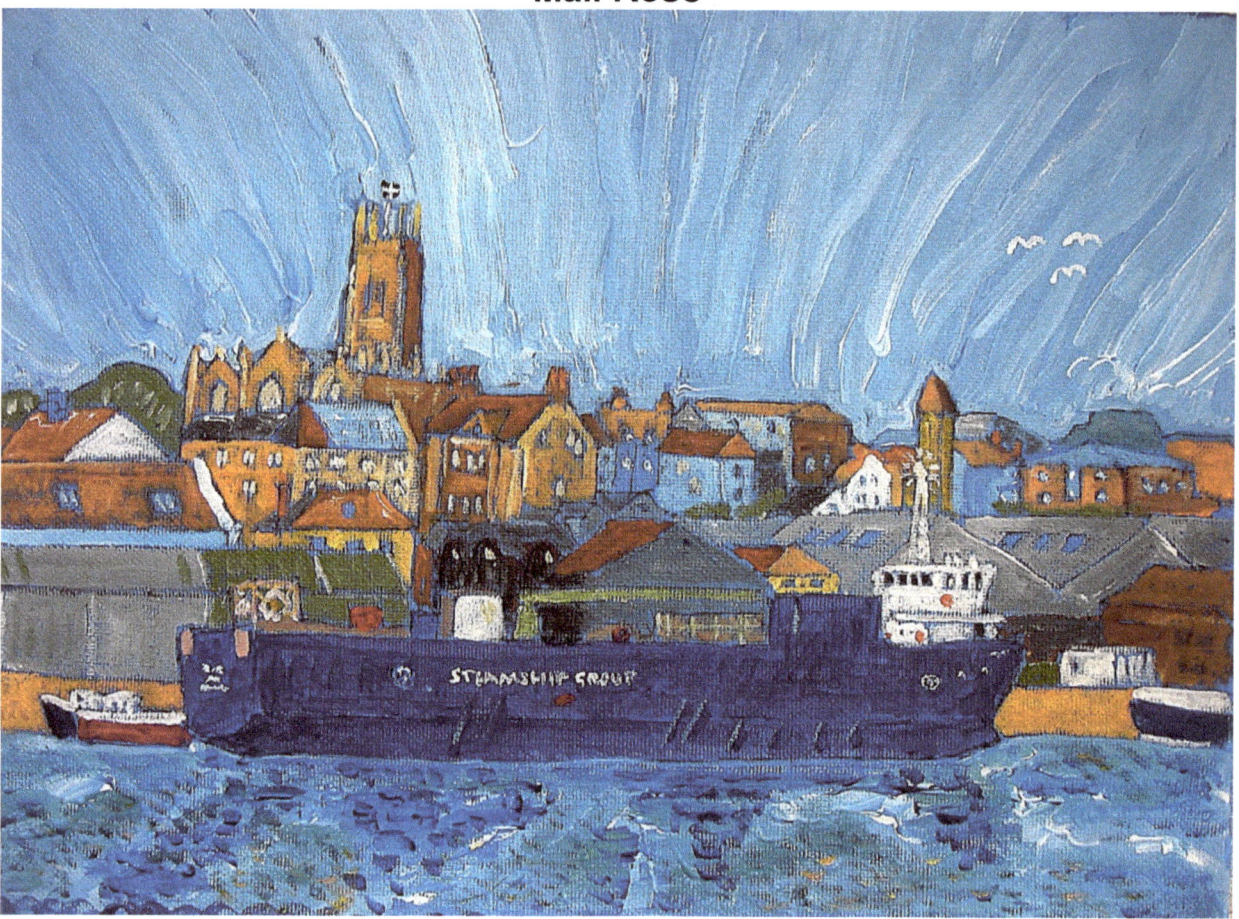

Mali Rose - *cargo vessel built in Norway in 1992 and sailed the fjords with fish meal as the main cargo. Acquired in 2016 by the steamship company to replace the Gry Maritha. A series of mishaps and conversions meant the vessel finally made her inaugural trial sailing on 17 July 2017 and provided a sporadic service before making her final voyage on 9 May 2019.*

Maria Assumpta

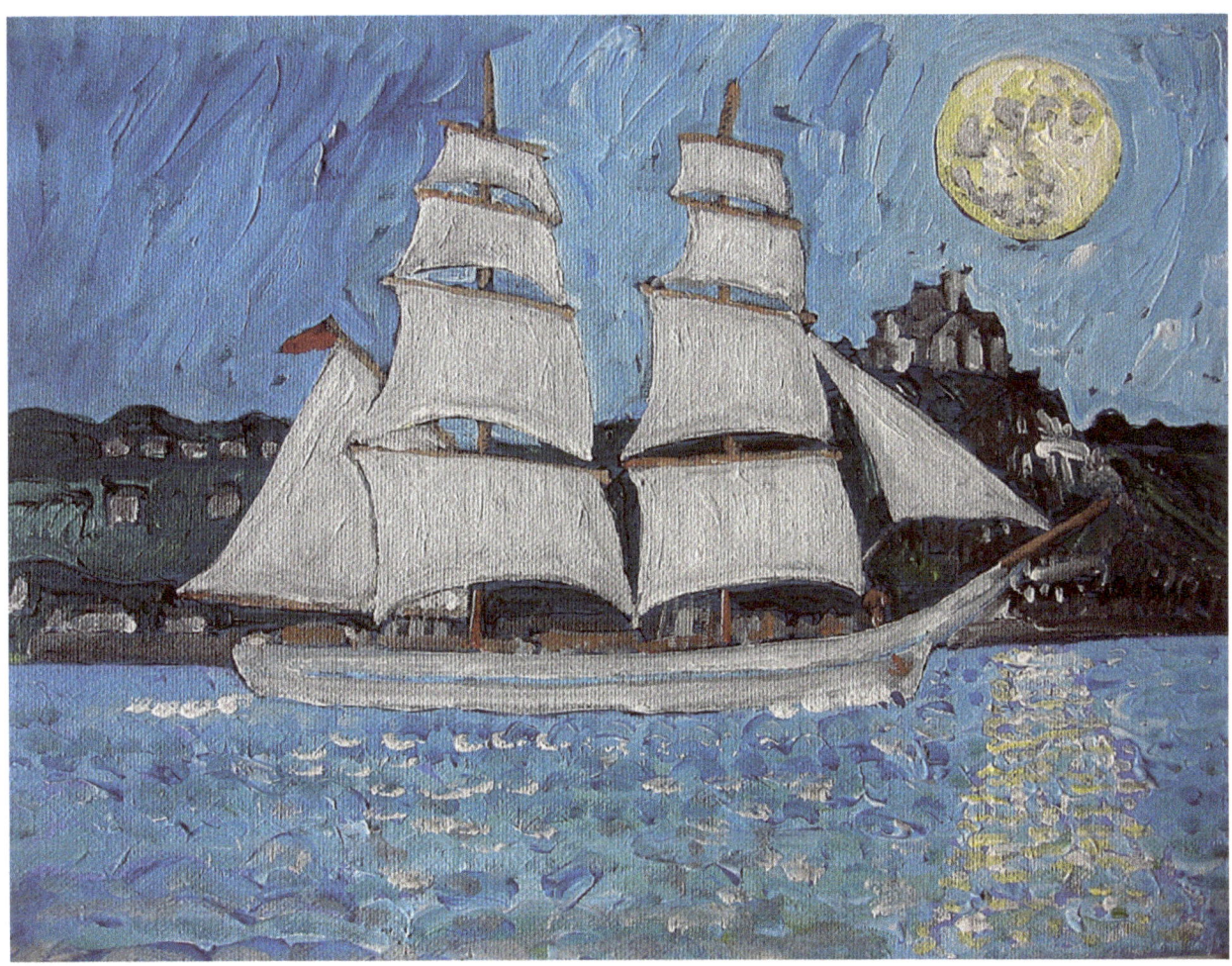

MARIA ASSUMPTA - built as brig or brigantine in Badalona, Spain for trading between Spain and Argentina transported wine, olive oil, grain and haberdashery, cane sugar, rum and tobacco until 1930. 05/30/95 lost on the coast of Cornwall (Rump Point), on her way to Golowan Sea and Sail, Penzance, because of technical problems with the engine and heavy drift, three people lost their lives.

Matthew

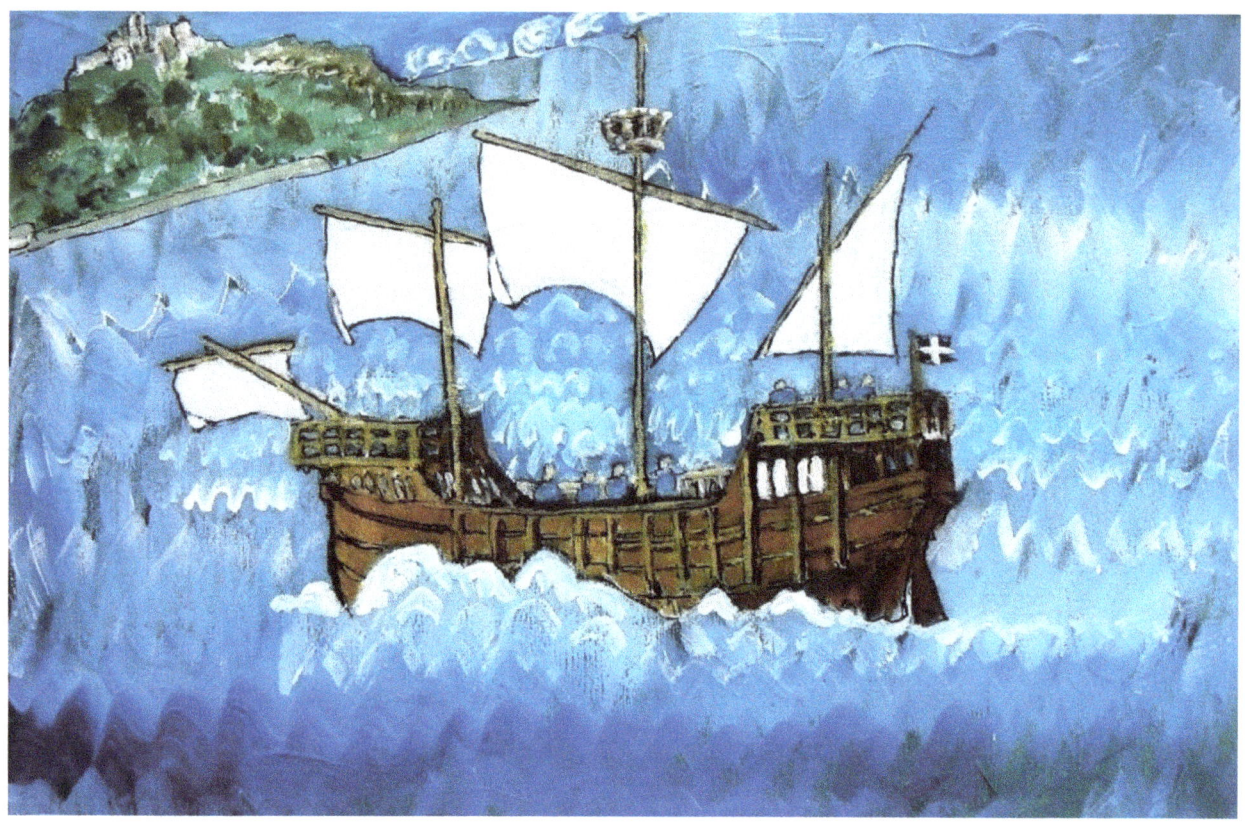

MATTHEW - In 1994 construction on a replica of *Matthew* began in a shipyard in Bristol. The replica measures 78 feet long, and is a faithful recreation of a 15th-century caravel of the era. The ship cost $3.8 million and took two years to build.

Maybe 2021

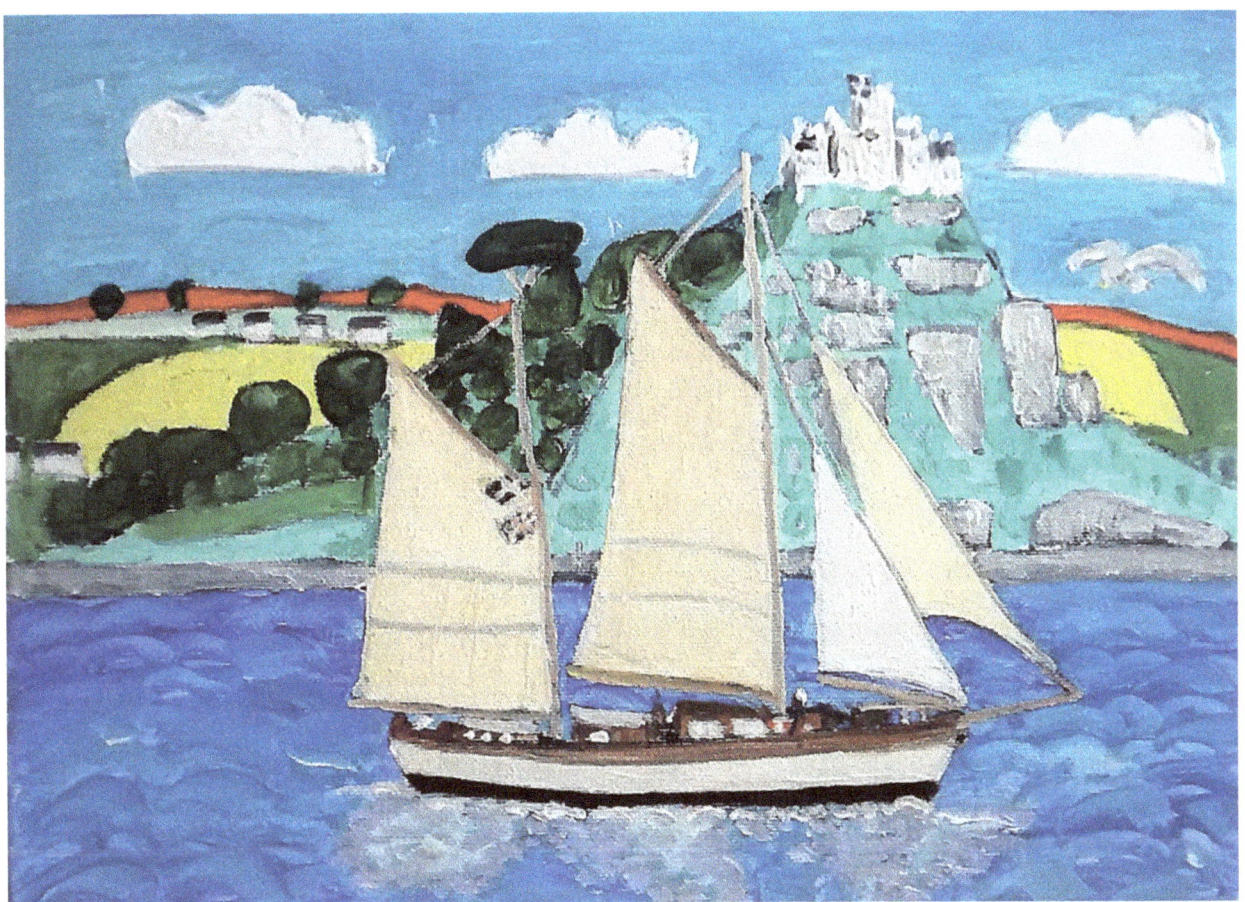

A major milestone in **MAYBE**'s history is that she took part in the first ever International Tall Ships Race in 1956. She is now one of the few boats that took part in that first race to still be competing in the International Tall Ship Races. A real claim to fame! In 1962, TS Maybe was bought by the Swiss family Hans Fehr, who were experienced sailors and enjoyed sailing in warmer climates. She sailed mainly around the Mediterranean and in the 1970s regularly crossed the Atlantic between the West Indies and the Mediterranean. IN the 1980s she also sailed through the Panama Canal and up the East coast of the USA to Canada. Tall ship Maybe was sold to her present owners in 1989 and underwent another complete restoration returning to sailing in 2007. She returned to the International Tall Ship Races in the Baltics in 2009. In 2011, TS Maybe was restored to her original gaff rig.

Mayflower

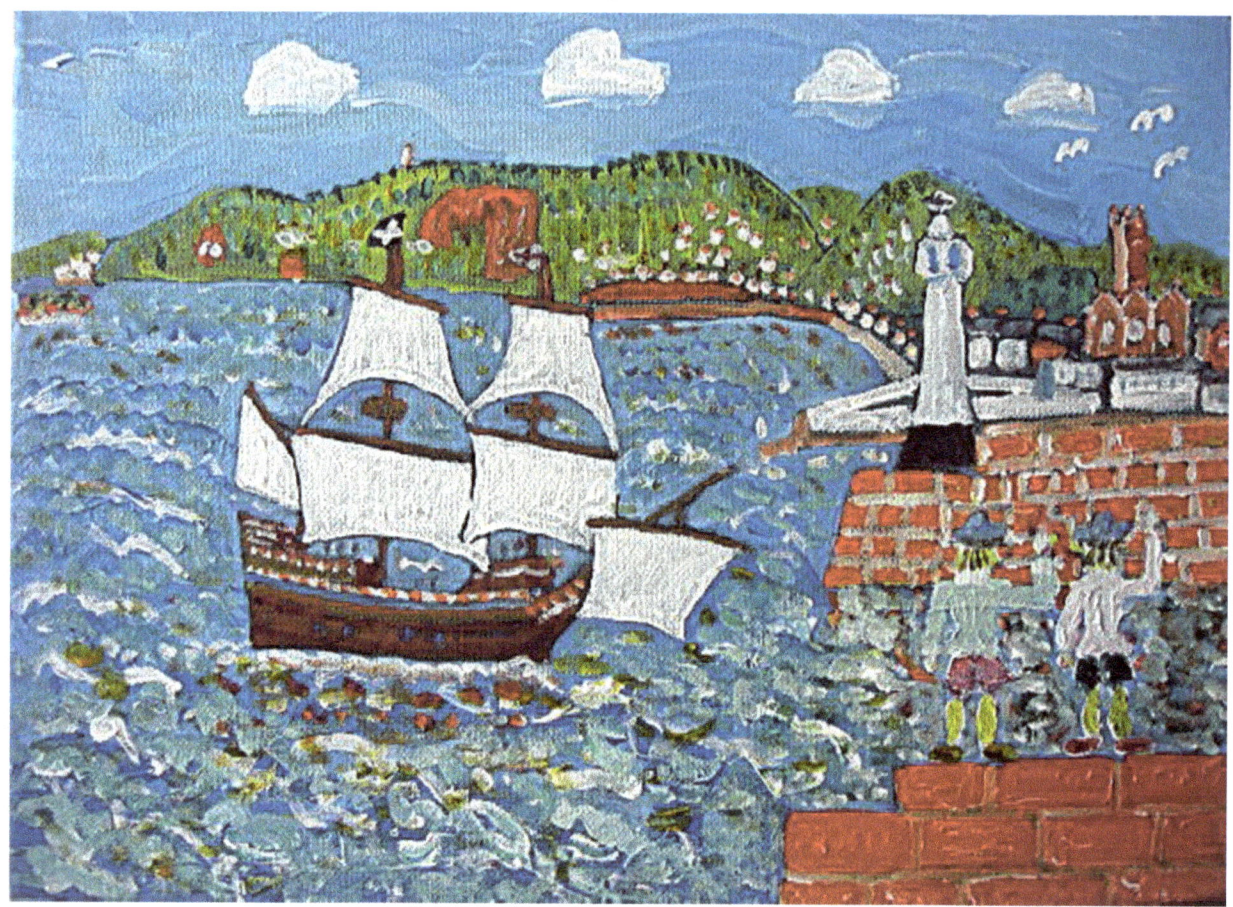

Mayflower 1620

THE MAYFLOWER - was built in 1590, although it is not known where, and was based in Harwich until 1610. Harwich was the home of Capt. Christopher Jones who led the Pilgrim Fathers voyage. His home is being converted into a museum ahead of the 400th anniversary.

Mez Creiz

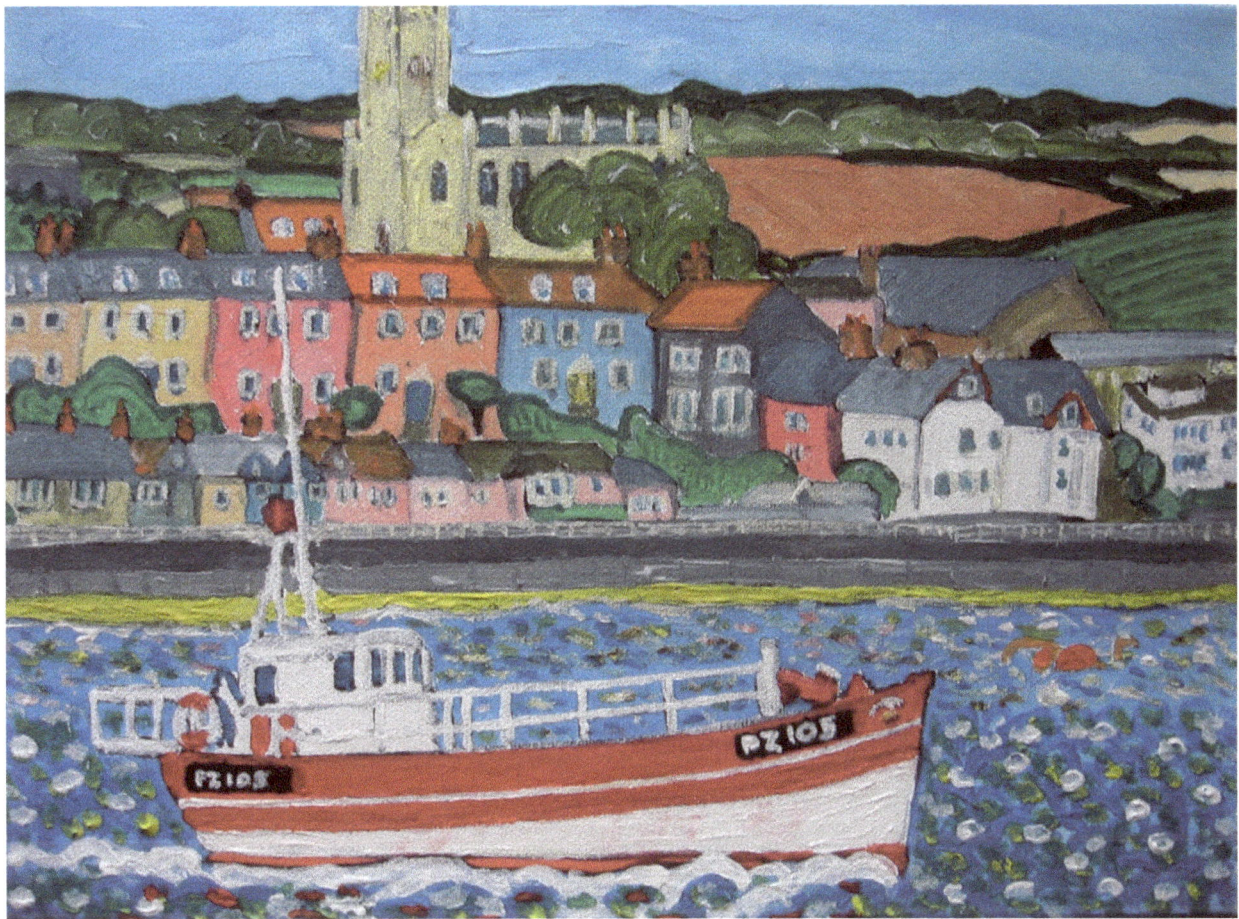

MEZ CREIS - in Newlyn, as a fishing vessel not long ago. (c2002). Official Number issued ON 362465 - Registry 11 March 1974; Appropriation 25 January 1975. Built at Camaret, France in 1954. French crabber.

Michael and Mary

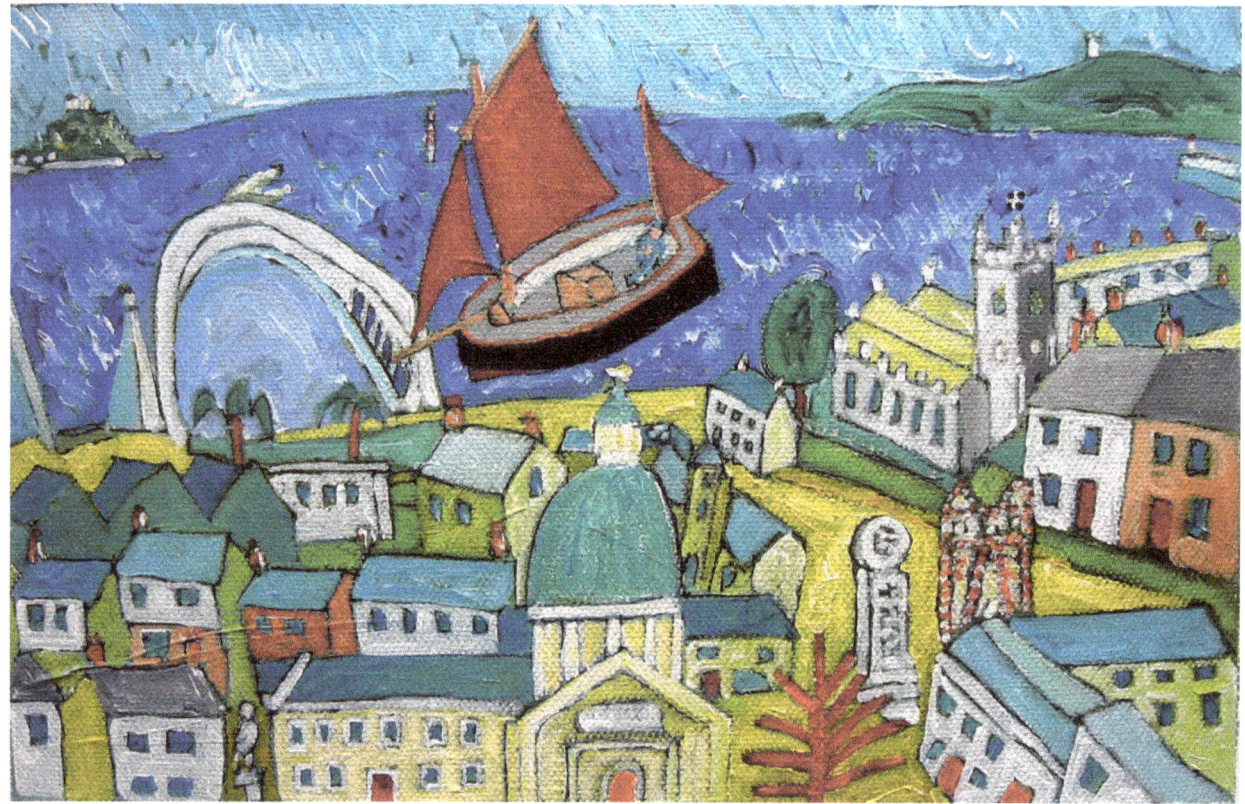

Michael and Mary, Penzance

MICHAEL AND MARY - Within the UK there are said to be two powerful Ley lines, the Michael and Mary lines. The Michael line, which was first mapped by John Mitchell, crosses England, from east to west, starting near Great Yarmouth, on the Norfolk coast, and ending at St Michael's Mount, on the western tip of Cornwall.

The Mary line is thought to be more meandering and entwines around the Michael line, meeting at certain points. Dowsers say that the energies they feel for each line are different. The Michael line is solar and masculine while the Mary line is lunar and feminine.

Mounts Bay

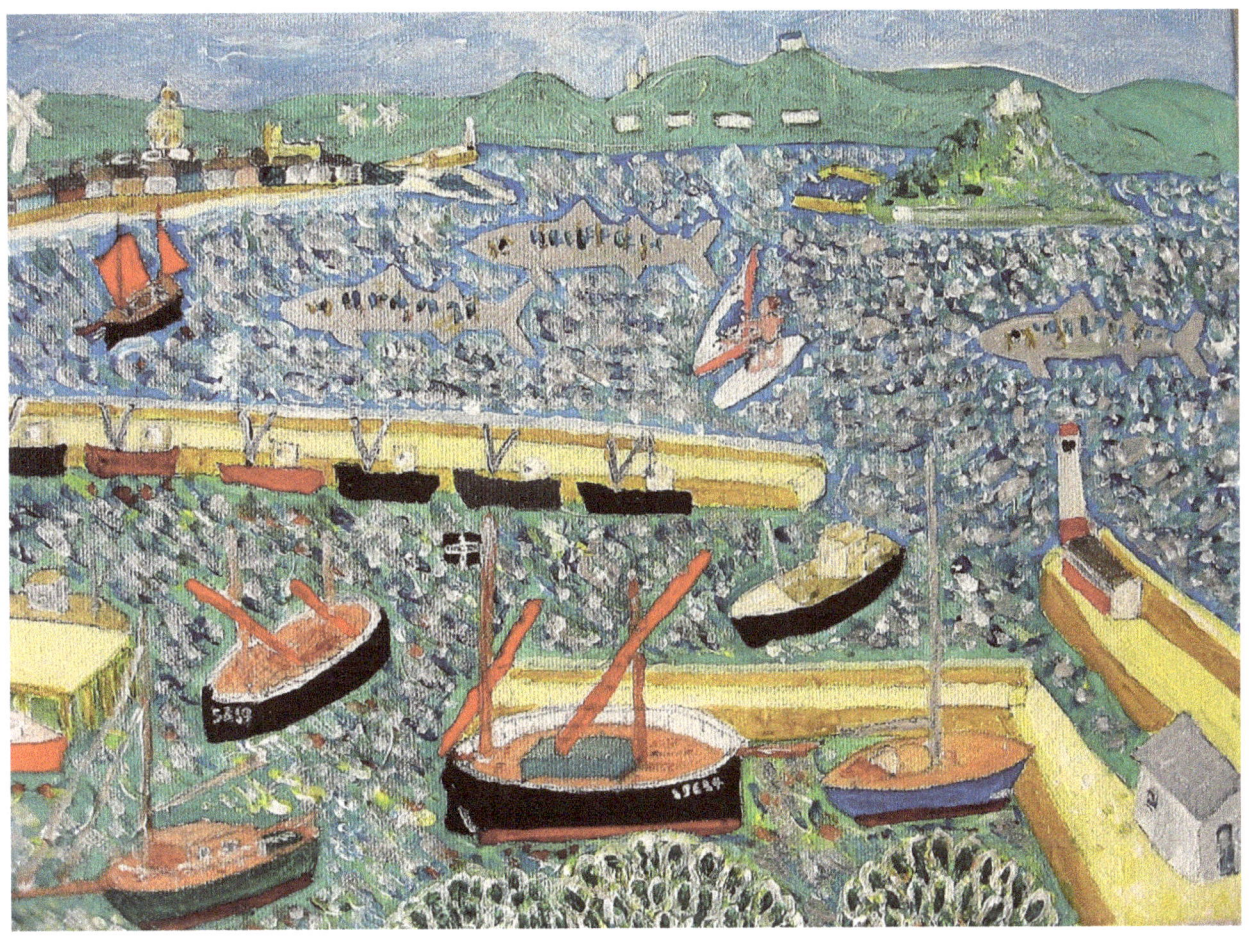

Morning Light, Mounts Bay

Nordlys

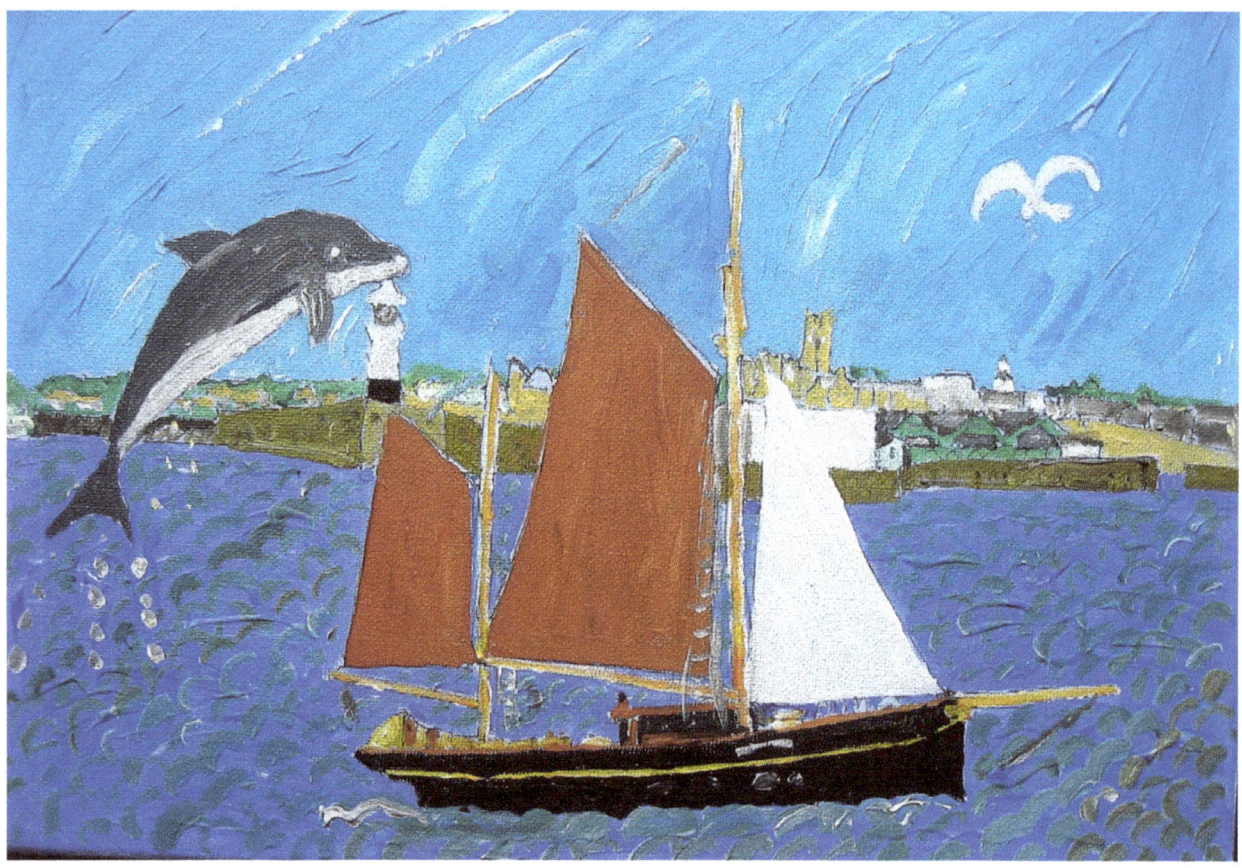

NORDLYS - She started her rich life in 1873, this wooden cutter is the oldest cargo ship still sailing. She brought the freshly caught fish from the fishing boats to the harbours as quickly as possible. She was built on the Isle of Wight, south of England. Nordlys was fully restored in 2014 and added to the fleet in 2015. Five voyages across European seas she has completed in complete safety.

Ocean Pride

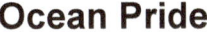

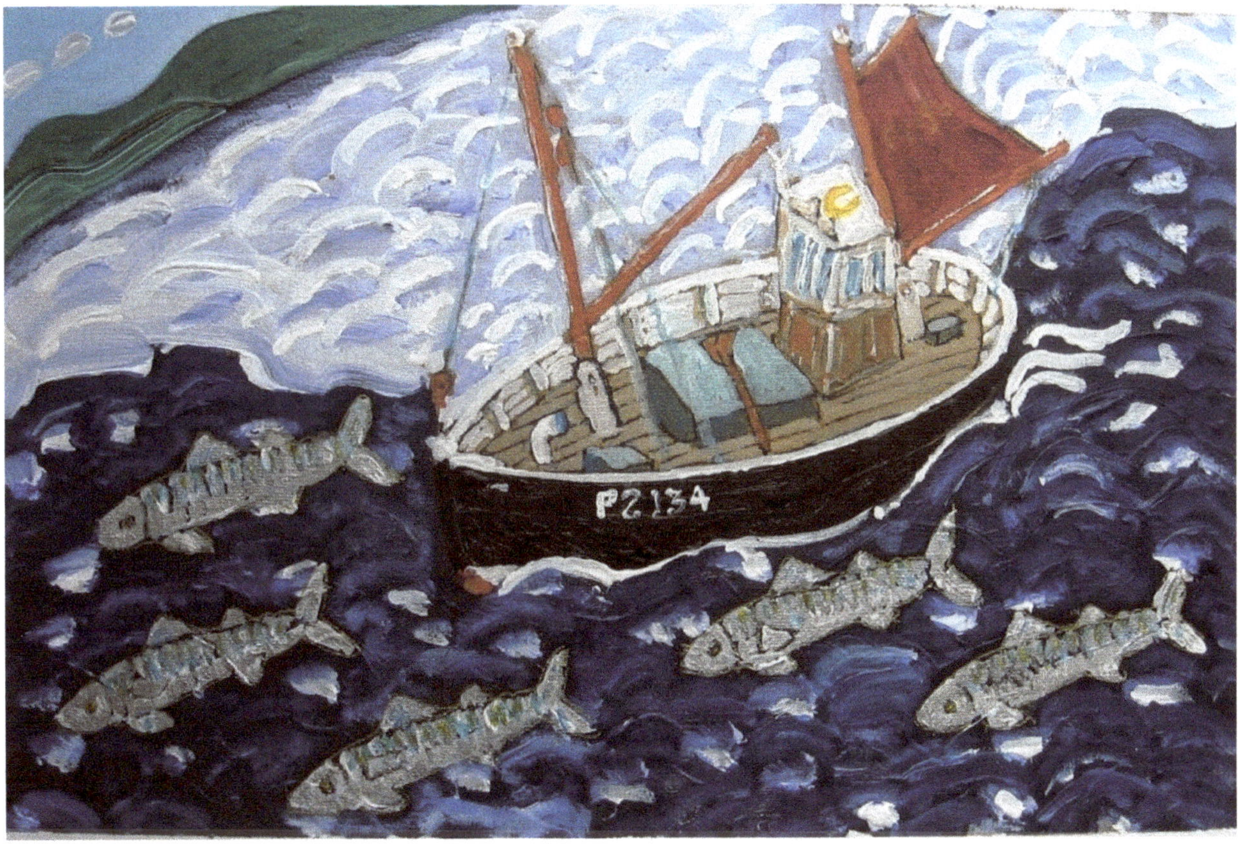

Mackerel Driver Ocean Pride

OCEAN PRIDE - is a Newlyn Lugger - a fishing vessel built by Henry Peake of Newlyn in 1919. She is of timber carvel construction and has a Badouin diesel engine of 108 hp, installed in 1975. The vessel is one of two known counter stern luggers in Mousehole and was decommissioned in 1991. She is believed to be the last remaining counter sterned Mounts Bay Lugger.

As of 2018, the vessel has been returned to Newlyn where she has been surveyed, fenced and housed for restoration and preservation.

Old Man of the Sea

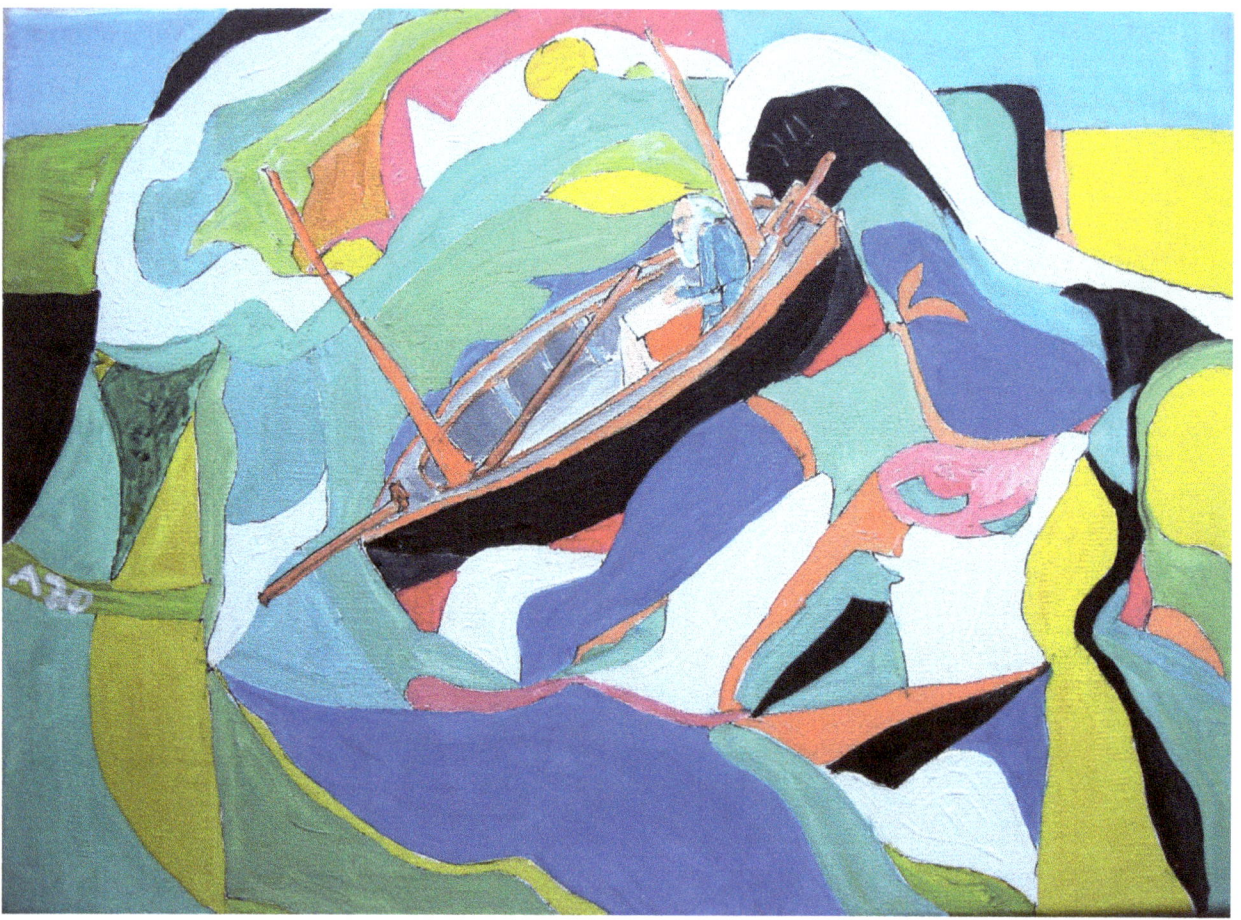

Sunrise over St Michaels Mount

St Michael's Mount (Cornish: Karrek Loos yn Koos, meaning "hoar rock in woodland") is a tidal island in Mount's Bay, Cornwall, England, United Kingdom. The island is a civil parish and is linked to the town of Marazion by a causeway of granite setts, passable (as is the beach) between mid-tide and low water. It is managed by the National Trust, and the castle and chapel have been the home of the St Aubyn family since around 1650.

Orion

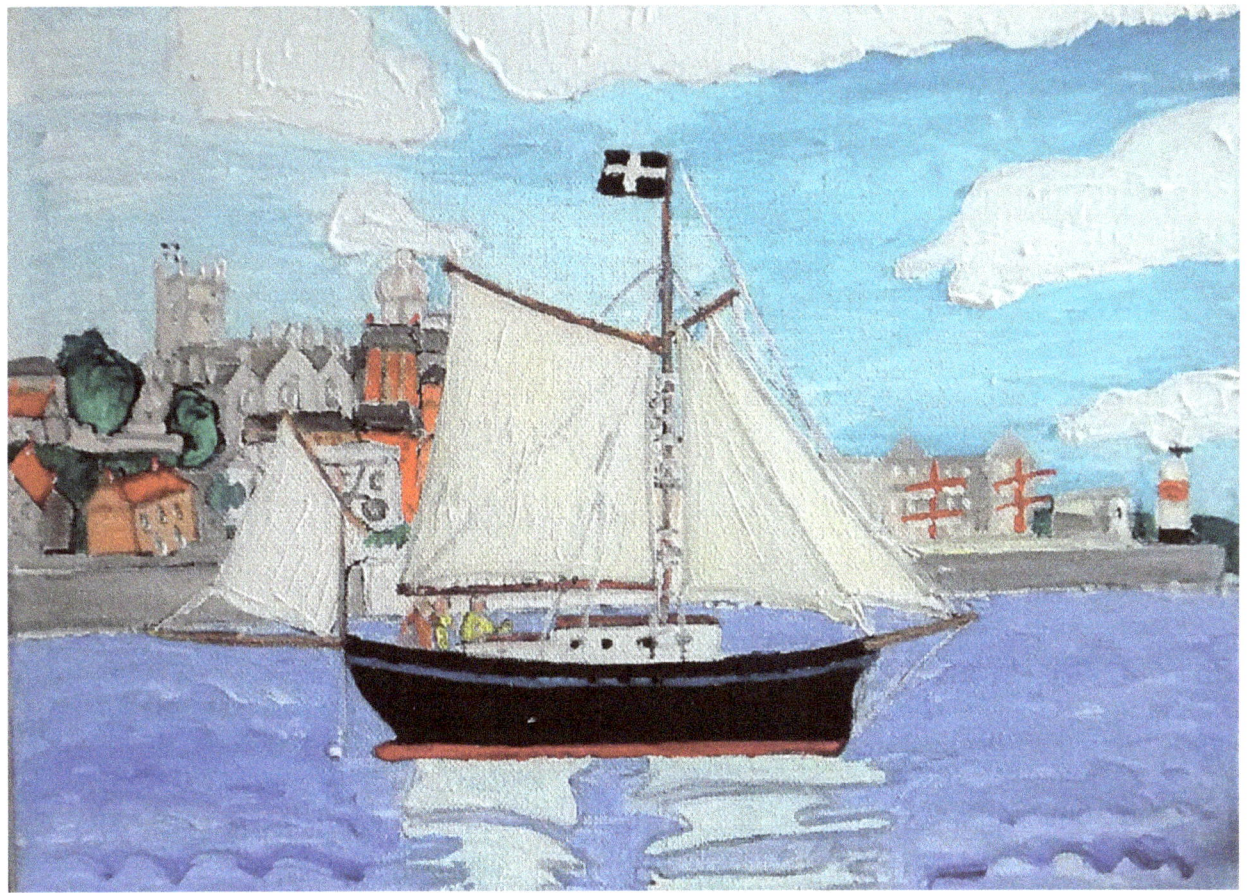

Orion approaching Penzance Harbour

Pet

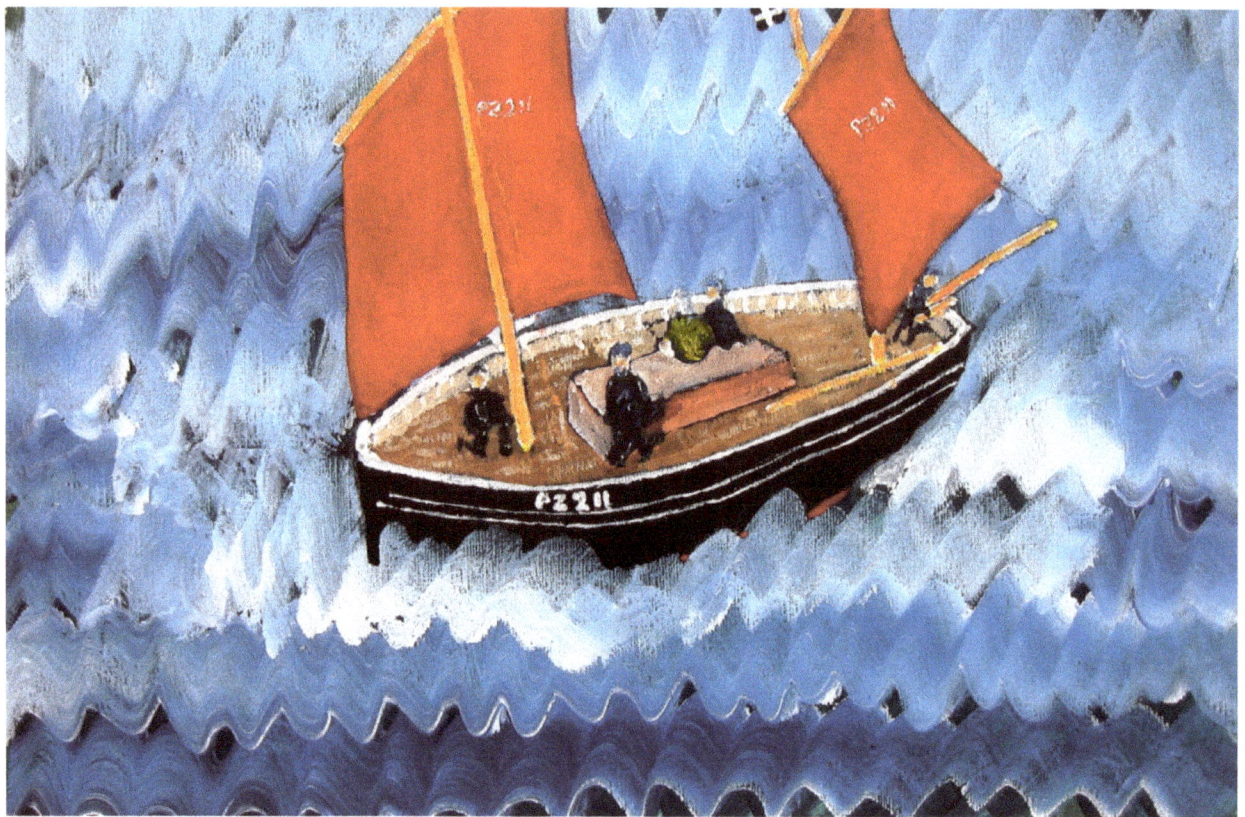

Pet PZ211

PET - is a Pilchard Driver built in 1903 in Porthleven for Richard Henry Thomas, who was born in 1863, Pet's first registration number was PZ211.

Pilchard Drivers were always known as fine, seaworthy vessels, and it is a privilege for us to have the opportunity to restore one of these fantastic craft back to her original working condition. Pet was being used as an engineless private yacht and whilst cruising in the Channel Islands in 2010 she dragged anchor and was wrecked just off the entrance of St. Peters Port. The wreck was later sold for £1 to a boatman at St Michaels Mount.

Penzance Harbour

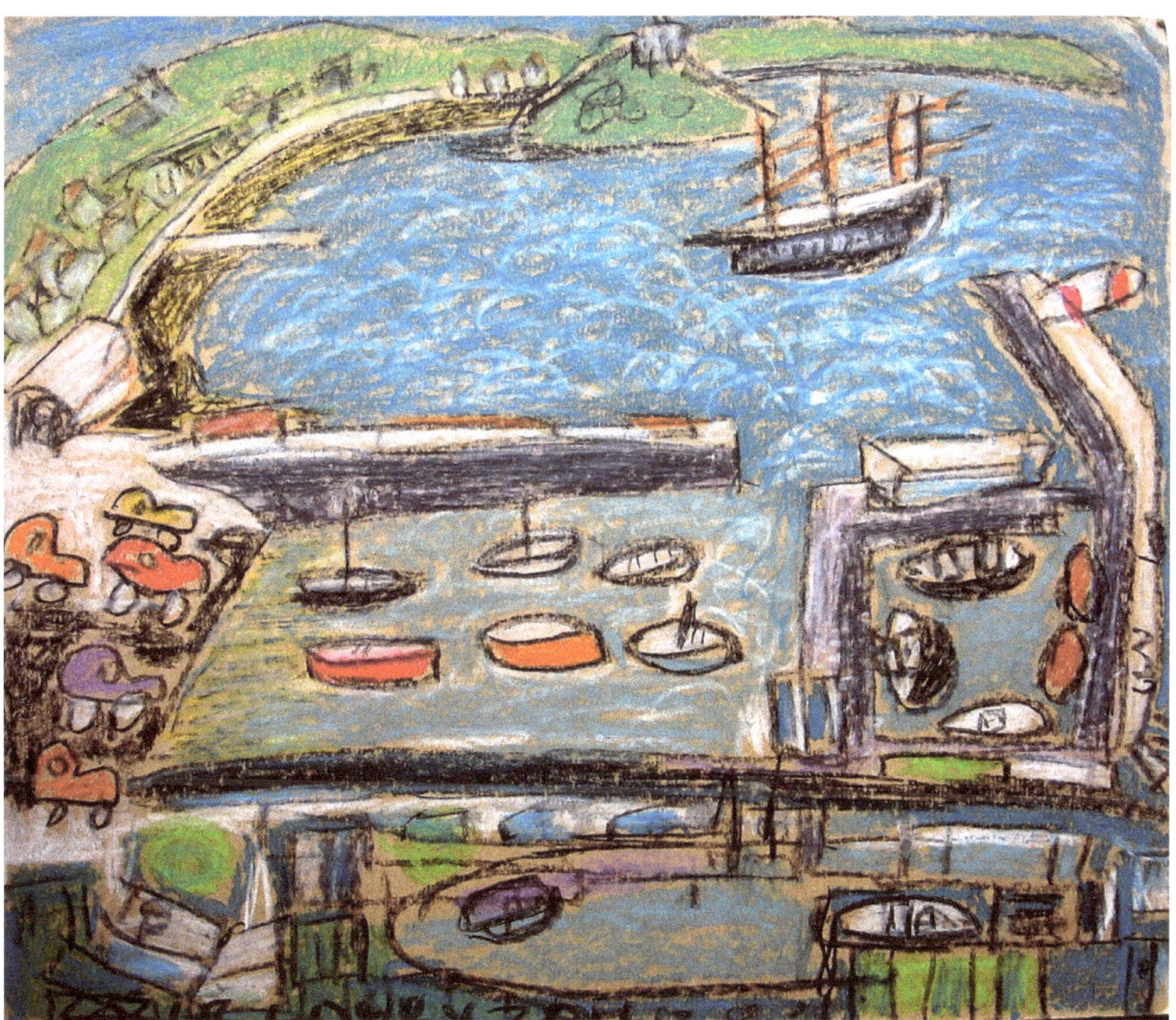

It is not known when the first quay was built at Penzance, but by the start of the 15th century it had six full-time fishing boats, and it had licensed ships ferrying pilgrims from St Michael's Mount to the shrine of St James of Compostella, in northwest Spain. The earliest record of a quay at Penzance comes from the time when Henry VIII granted it harbour dues, but it also referred to repair works of an existing 15th-century structure.

Phoenix

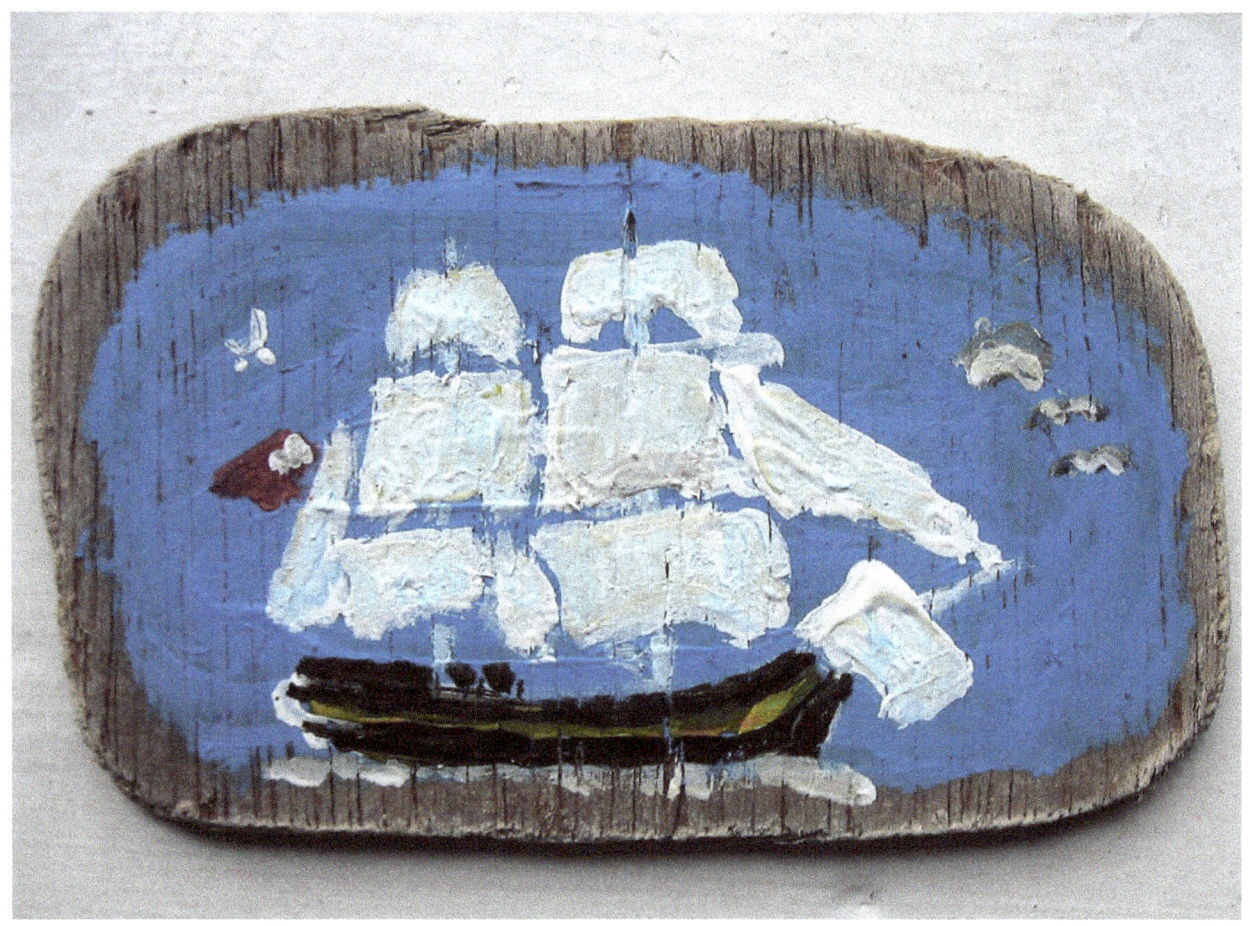

Acrylic on driftwood 5x3"

SEA SERPENTS
I am often asked about the presence of sea serpents in my pictures. Of course they are only there if they want to be! From mind to canvas-borrowed not stolen. There is very little we know about the oceans, other than us monsters are polluting them affecting all the sea creatures. There is much to be discovered. Giant mackerel, dolphins and gulls also appear. The sea dragon off Lands End often has her flames mistaken for the sunset, and only appears when she is placing her eggs where she wants them to hatch. The sea serpents that appear in the pictures are benign creatures, whose job it is to look after the maritime issues of Penzance and Mounts Bay. They are mister with the blue chest and missus with the white one.

Queen of the Bay

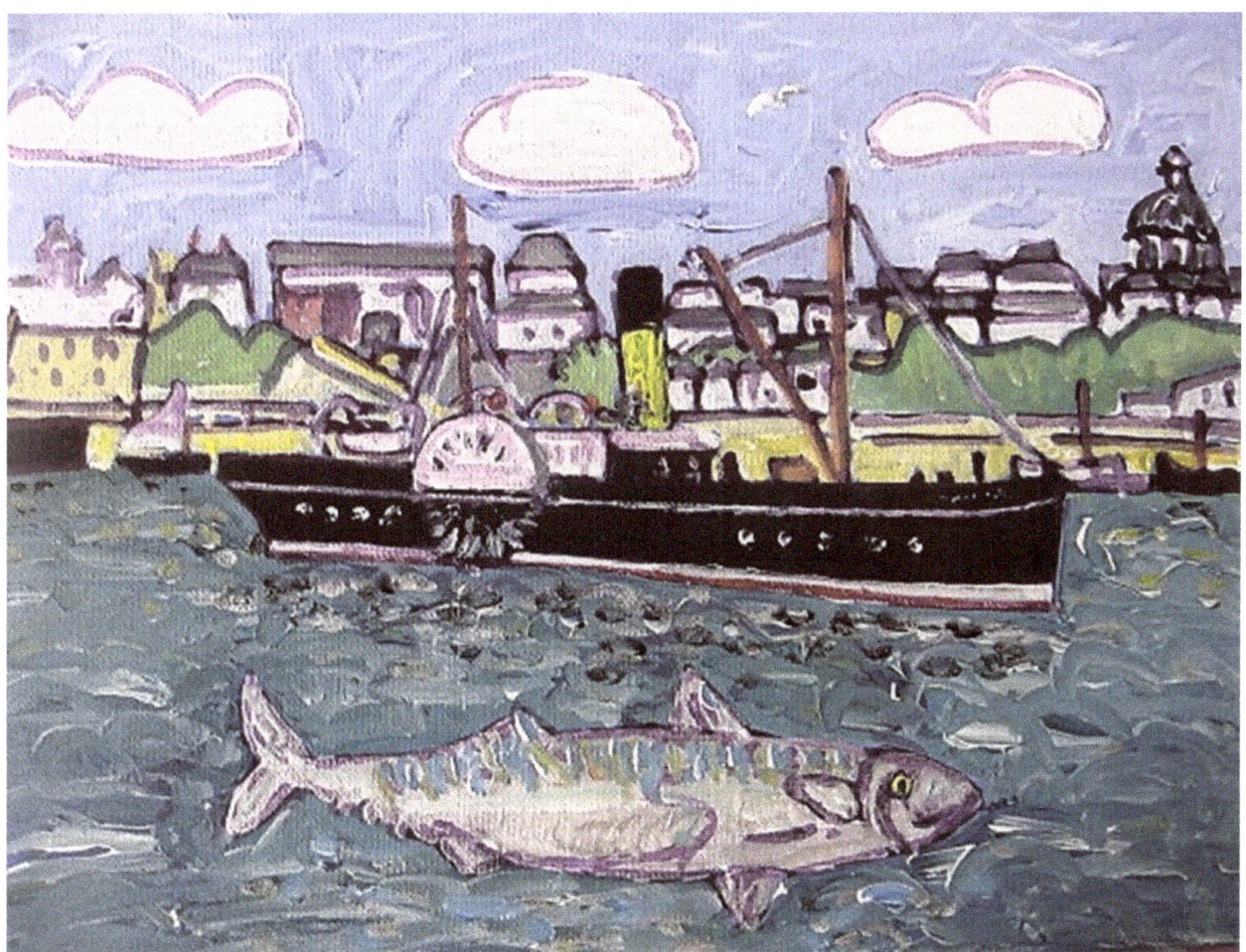

QUEEN OF THE BAY - was a passenger vessel operated by the West Cornwall Steam Ship Company from 1873 to 1885. She was built by Henderson Coulborn and Company in Renfrew and launched in 1867. She operated for the Blackpool, Lytham and Southport Steam Packet Company out of Morecambe for five years and then Blackpool for two years.

SV Nicolai

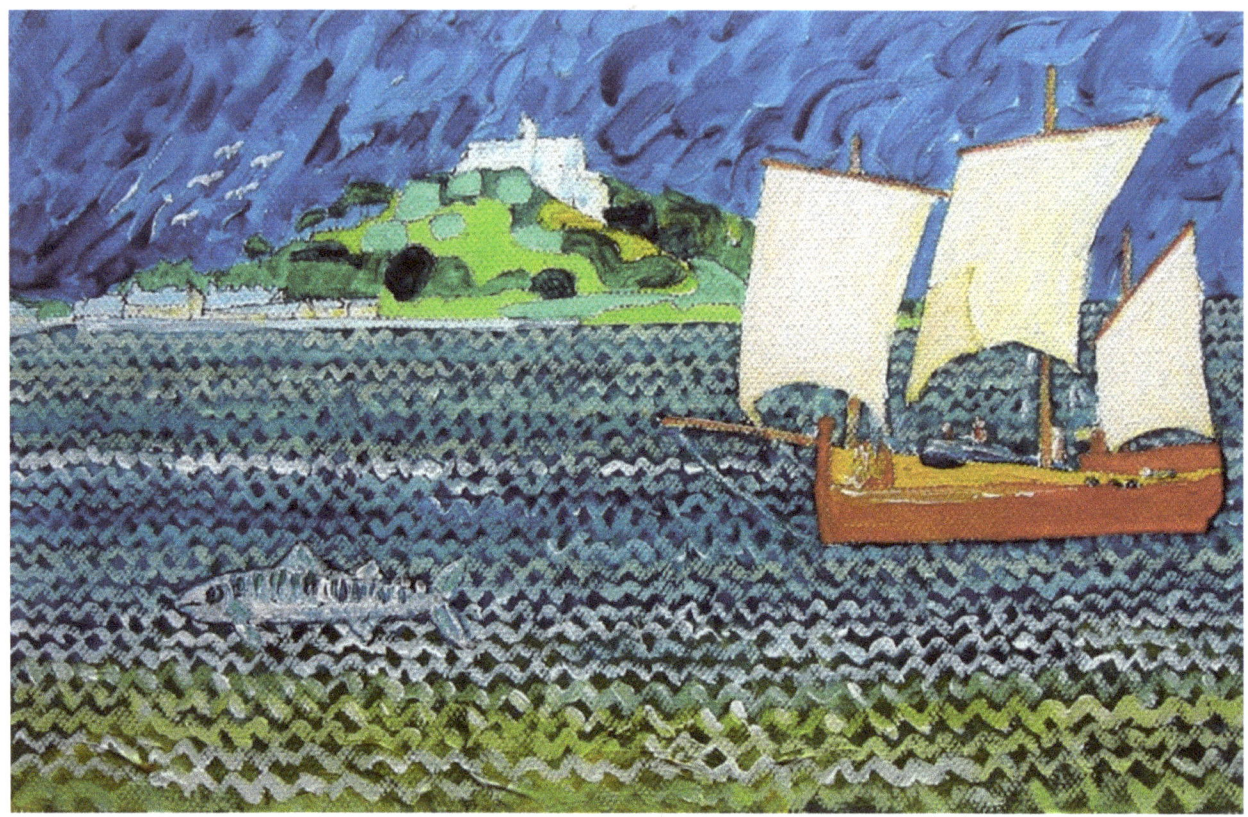

NICOLAI - is a replica of a Russian cargo vessel sailed to Penzance for Golowan Sea and Sail by a crew including the Archbishop of St Petersburg.

Thalassa

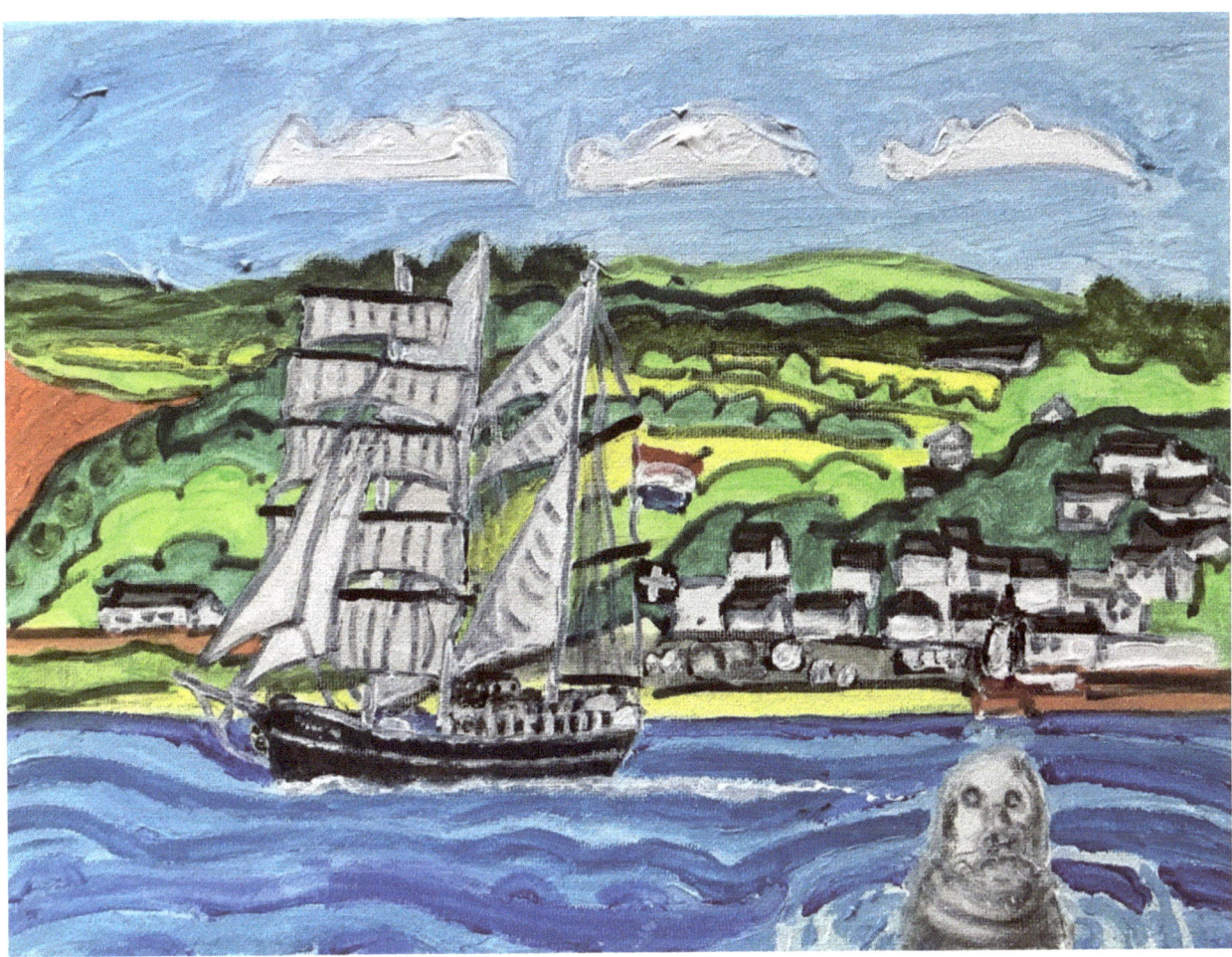

Thalassa - is a 50m class A rigged according to old traditions. launched in 1980. Barquentine Thalassa is an imposing and seaworthy tall ship. This three master is one of the most beautiful and fastest sea sailers of the Dutch fleet. Rigged according to old traditions, Thalassa is fitted with all modern safety conveniences and perfectly combines adventurous sailing with comfortable enjoyment.

The Bag o' Rags

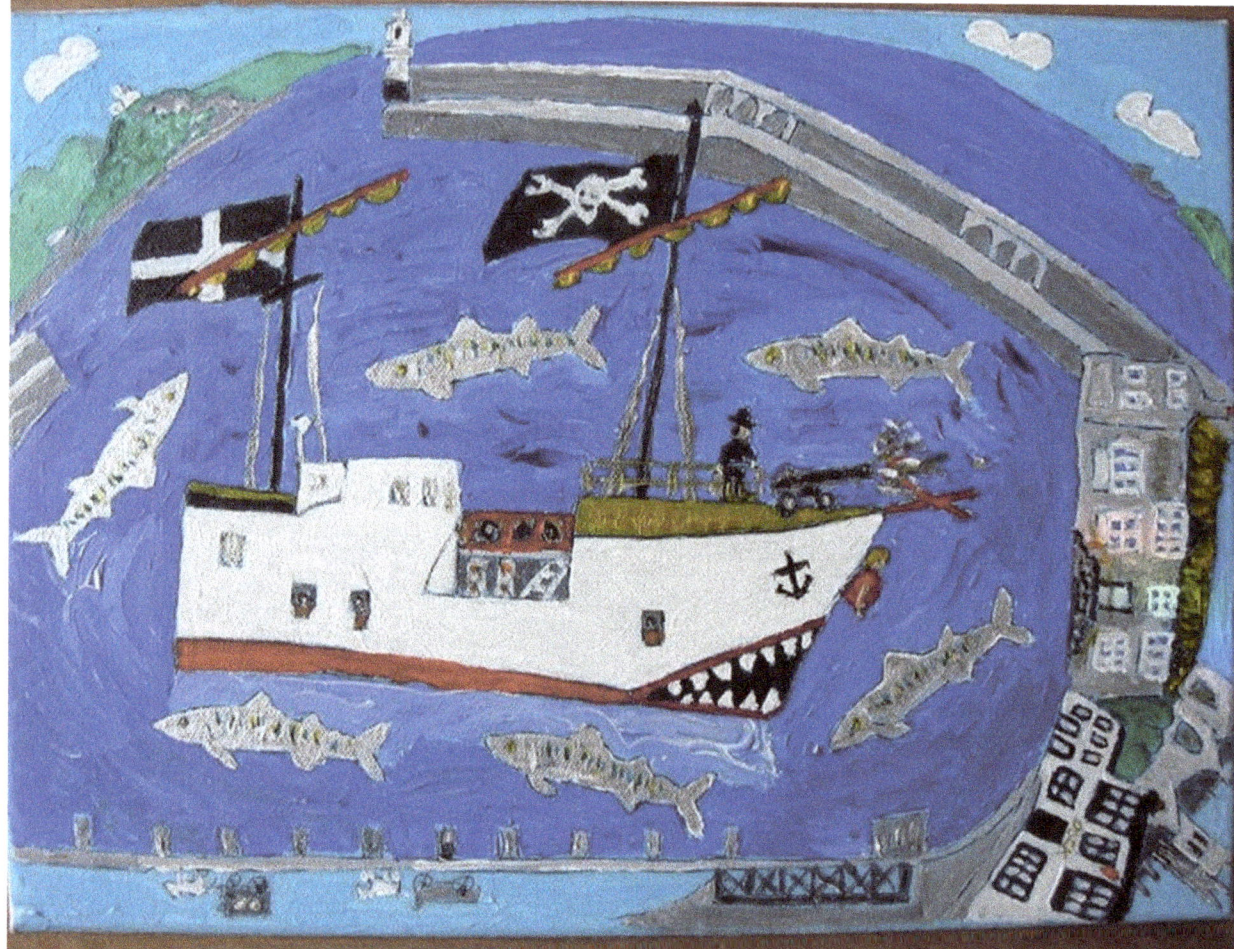

Mackerel (Scomber scombrus) are a small, fast predatory fish which is common around almost all of the British Isles in the summer months.

A former fishing boat which was turned into a floating pirate shop has sunk in Penzance harbour in the wake of Storm Antoni. The sad demise of the vessel comes after a remarkable career which began in the early 70s when the Ar Bageergan - which means 'the eye of the wind' - worked as a tuna boat and crabber off the French coast, having been built in Brittany in the early 1970s. However she was later sold to a Newlyn fisherman who worked her until 2000 as a drift netter catching cod off the Irish coast, hake in the South West and tuna in the Bay of Biscay.

The Black Pig

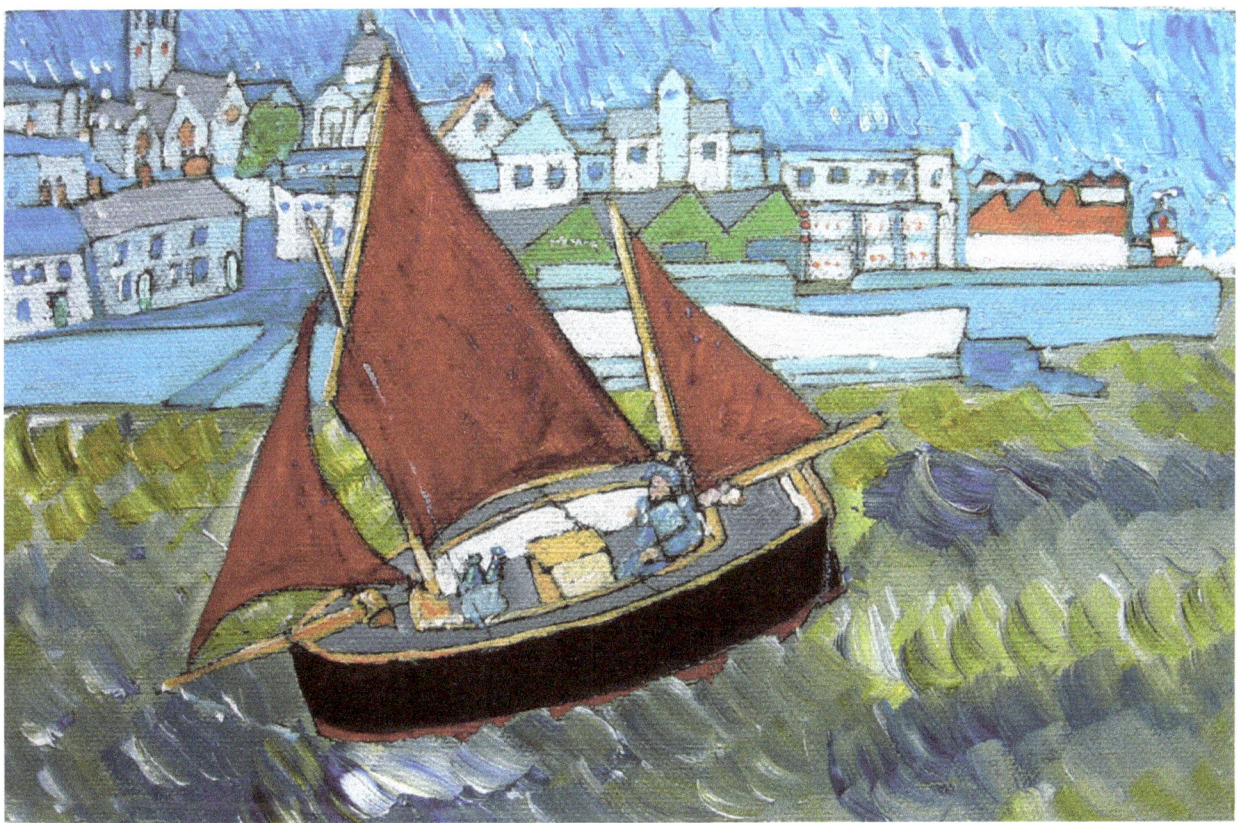

An Hogh Dhu, Mucky conditions off Penzance

THE BLACK PIG - Terry Heard Lug Rigged Mevagissey Tosher AN HOGH DHU, (ex ALANNA) sail number **T2**. Built in 1975 by Terry Heard for himself. Lug mainsail, foresail and mizzen, with inboard Petter mini 6 and sweeps. Main mast 20ft, mizzen 12ft. A working tosher.

Veryan in the wet dock

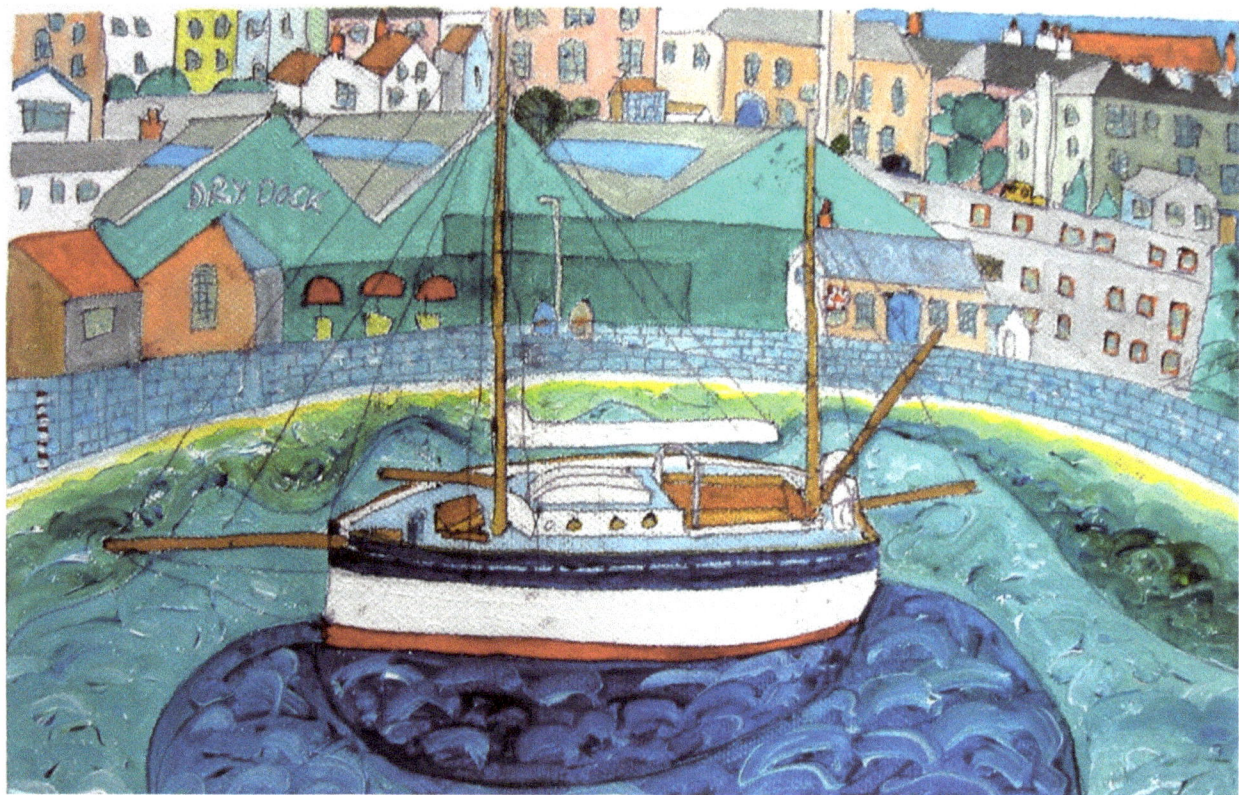

VERYAN - Living relics from a bygone age, the Falmouth Working Boats make an impressive sight, and there can be few who are not inspired by the beauty of these powerful gaff-rigged cutters under sail. Outwardly, little has changed in nearly 200 years, their existence being a direct result of the local harbour byelaws prohibiting the dredging of oysters by any mechanical means. Working under sail and oar during the winter months from October to March, these unique boats have survived to become the last of their kind in Europe.

White boat

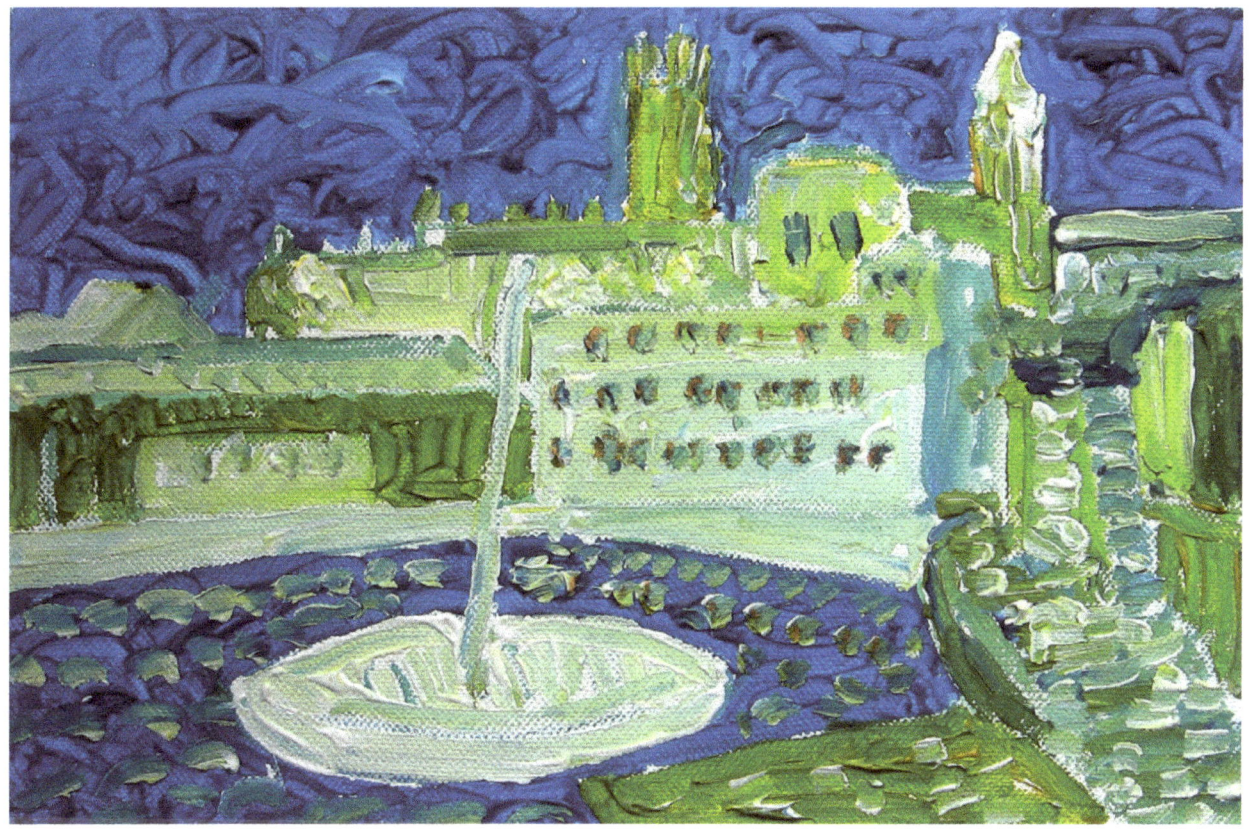

White boat Abbey Basin

Information Source Table

Page	Description	Source/reference	Year painted
4	Out Of The World		2023
11	Abbey Basin	https://historicengland.org.uk/listing/the-list/list-entry/1393737?	2023
12	Asgaardii -	https://en.wikipedia.org ›wiki › Asgaard_II	2019
13	Astrid -	https://en.wikipedia.org/wiki/STV_Astrid	2017
14	Barnabas -	http://cornishmaritimetrust.org/barnabas/	2021
15	Bessie Ellen - Pellew	https://bessie-ellen.com › history/ https://venturesailholidays.com/ship/pilot-cutter-pellew/	2023
16	Bessie Ellen	https://bessie-ellen.com › history	2017
17	Blue Clipper -	*https://www.maybe-sailing.com › ship › blue-clipper*	2023
18	Breton Crabbers -	https://fishingnews.co.uk/features/refit-to-vivier-crabber-pen-glas/	2017
19	Captain Ahab -	https://www.britannica.com › topic › Captain-Ahab	2017
20	Carlos De Amesquita	https://en.wikipedia.org/wiki/Carlos_de_Amésquita	2010
21	Corydalis - Is	https://garyball.blogspot.com	2010
22	Courier	https://www.shipsnostalgia.com/media/russian-replica-replica-of-corvette-quot-courier	2010
23	Crazy Diamond -	https://en.wikipedia.org/wiki/Shine_On_You_Crazy_Diamond	2019
24	De Gallant,	https://fairtransport.eu/en/our-fleet/the-gallant/.	2020
25	Dragon Fly - Brin	https://www.superyachtfan.com › nl › yacht › dragonfly › owner	2019
26	Dream Boat	https://www.etymonline.com › word › dreamboat	2012
27	The Earl Of Pembroke -	https://www.westerntelegraph.co.uk/news/23199681.pembroke-dock-mourns-loss-earl-pembroke-ship/	2019
28	Elizabeth And Blanche Ii	https://penleehouse.org.uk/object/pezph-1989-622/	2020
29	Ellian - Last Sailing Vessel Delivering Coal From Cardiff 1955, Wales, And Elian. Involved In The Coastal Trade.		2019
30	Evening View		2020
31	Excelsior -	https://theexcelsiortrust.co.uk/excelsior	2019
32	The Eye Of The Wind	https://www.eyeofthewind.net/en/ship/history	2019
33	Feasible -	https://www.nationalhistoricships.org.uk/register/711/feasible	2014
34	Ghost Ship - Painted In Memory Of Local Artist Breon O'casey.		2017
35	Gleaner -	https://www.nationalhistoricships.org.uk/register/2750/gleaner# http://www.porthlevenmuseum.org.u	2023
36	Golden Hind -	https://en.wikipedia.org/wiki/Golden_Hind#	2019
37	Grace -	https://www.nationalhistoricships.org.uk › register › 109 › grace	2010
38	Grayhound -	https://tallshipsnetwork.com/vessels/grayhound/	2014
39	Grossherzogin Elisabeth -	https://sailtraininginternational.org/vessel/grossherzogin-elisabeth/	2013
40	Gry Maritha -	https://en.wikipedia.org/wiki/Gry_Maritha	2019
41	Guide Me -	https://www.nationalhistoricships.org.uk/register/2149/guide-me	2014
42	Gulliver	https://en.wikipedia.org/wiki/Gulliver%27s_Travels	2017
43	Happy Return Is A Cornish Lugger Built		2018
44	Happy Return	www.happyreturn.org	2010
45	Hear The Sea.	Can you hear the waves?	2012
45	Storms	https://www.bbc.co.uk › news › uk-england-26028576	2014
46	Herring Gull	https://www.wildlifetrusts.org › wildlife-explorer › birds › seabirds › herring-gull	2014
47	Irene -	https://www.ireness.com/history/	2017
48	Johanna Lucretia -	https://www.theislandtrust.org.uk/boats/johanna-lucretia/	2019

49	John's Boys - In Porthleven.	https://eoceanic.com/sailing/harbours/564/porthleven_harbour	2010
50	Juno -	https://woodenships.co.uk/sailing-yacht/percy-dalton-tosher/	2020
51	[Kara Mor And] Karina Olsen -	https://blog.through-the-gaps.co.uk/2014/10/who-can-identify-karina-olsen.html	2020
52	Kinsmen Of The Wind -	https://www.americanpoems.com/poets/emilydickinson/the-duties-of-the-wind-are-few/	2014
53	Klevia -	https://angleseytraditionalsail.co.uk/klevia/	2022
54	The Lady Of Avenel	https://www.ladyofavenel.com	2018
55	Le Belem.	https://sailtraininginternational.org/vessel/belem/	2012
56	Little Gem & Minerva	https://www.picturepenzance.com/media/little-gem.9540/ https://www.youtube.com/watch?v=R1elw570nhM	2008
57	Longship-In		2023
58	The Lugger -	https://nmmc.co.uk/object/boats/cornish-luggers/	2011
58	Mounts Bay	https://en.wikipedia.org/wiki/Mount%27s_Bay	
58	Cape Cornwall	https://www.capecornwallgigclub.co.uk/home	
59	Luke's Minie	http://www.seasalts.co.uk/the-boats/lukes-minnie/	2008
60	Mali Rose Gry Maritha .	https://en.wikipedia.org › wiki › Isles_of_Scilly_Steamship_Company	2019
61	Maria Assumpta -	http://www.tallship-fan.de/cgi-bin/tallship_e.pl	2019
62	Matthew -	https://www.atlasobscura.com/places/the-matthew-replica-of-cabots-ship-that-sailed-to-newfoundland-in-1497	2010
63	Maybe	https://www.maybe-sailing.com/ship/maybe/	2021
64	The Mayflower -	https://www.bbc.co.uk/news/uk-england-essex-48267651	2019
65	Mez Creis -	https://www.picturepenzance.com/media/mez-creis-pz-105.9393/	2014
66	Michael And Mary -	https://www.roystoncave.co.uk/post/ley-lines	2011
67	Mount's Bay	https://en.wikipedia.org/wiki/Mount%27s_Bay	2020
68	Nordlys -	*https://fairtransport.eu › Our fleet*	2018
69	Ocean Pride	https://www.nationalhistoricships.org.uk/register/2390/ocean-pride	2010
70	Old Man Of The Sea	https://en.wikipedia.org/wiki/St_Michael%27s_Mount	2011
71	Orion -	is the smallest square sail vessel, Orion, The smallest square sail vessel in the UK owned by a local boat builder ans rigger.	2021
72	Pet -	http://butlerandco.blogspot.com/2011/11/pet.html	2010
73	Penzance Harbour		2012
74	Phoenix		2019
75	Queen Of The Bay - W	https://infogalactic.com›info › PS_Queen_of_the_Bay_(1867)	2019
76	Sv Nicolai		2010
77	Thalassa	https://tallshipsnetwork.com/vessels/thalassa/	2023
78	The Bag O'rags	https://www.cornwalllive.com/news/cornwall-news/pirate-ship-attacked-spanish-fisherman-8658351	2014
79	The Black Pig -	https://www.facebook.com/groups/2308220396109342/posts/2854978618100181/	2017
80	Veryan -	https://fwba.co.uk/our-boats/	2021
81	White Boat		2009

The Author

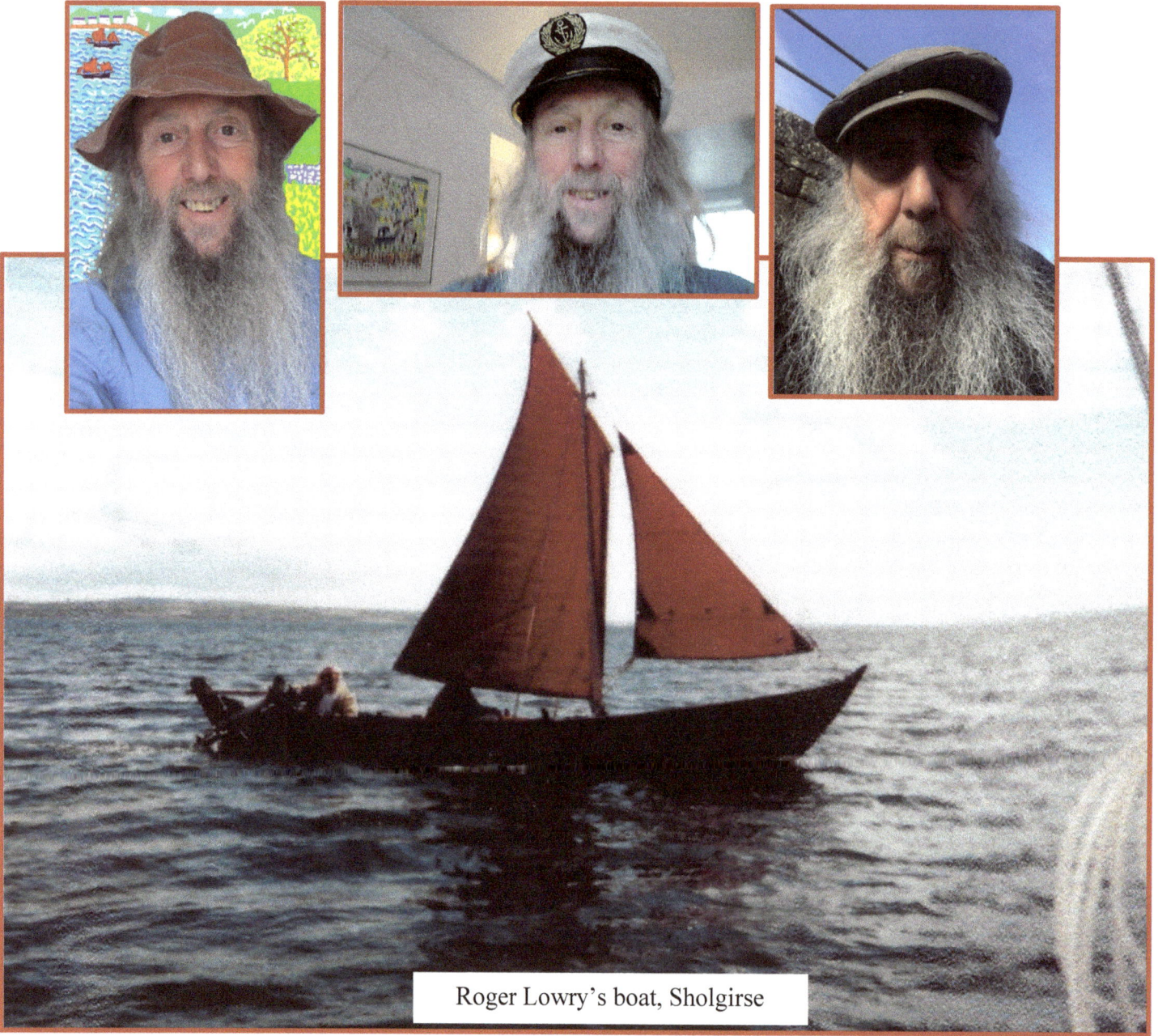

Roger Lowry's boat, Sholgirse

Book review

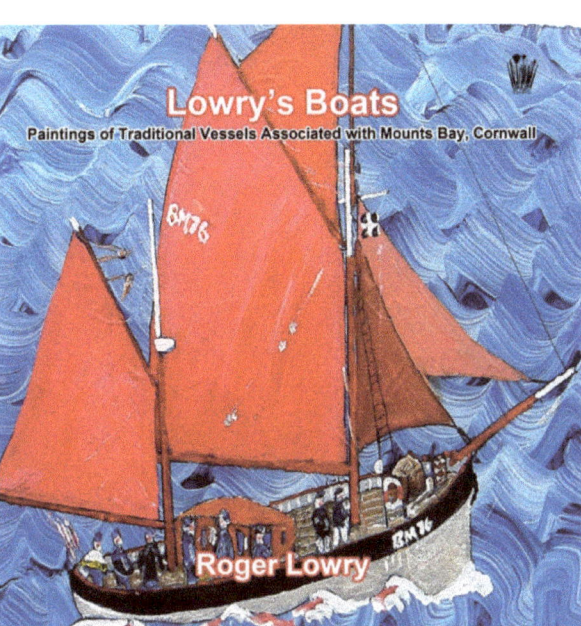

"Roger has made his own rules for his artistic expression, following in the footsteps of Alfred Mullins and Fred Yates. The vibrant use of colour hits you when looking at Roger's work. The use of impasto on some subjects gives a textual quality which lifts the work.

The naïve style of painting gives a licence to use colour in a way that conventional artists would not use. Every page is packed with colour that jumps out of the book.

I particularly liked the history index of the vessels portrayed in the book - it is packed with good information."

Rob Dennis
He is an artist and carver of figure heads for boats and is a member of the South West Maritime History Society.

Roger Lowry

www.ingramcontent.com/pod-product-compliance
Lightning Source LLC
Chambersburg PA
CBHW040543220526
45473CB00016B/3009